Christ's Under-Shepherds

Australian College of Theology Monograph Series

SERIES EDITOR GRAEME R. CHATFIELD

The ACT Monograph Series, generously supported by the Board of Directors of the Australian College of Theology, provides a forum for publishing quality research theses and studies by its graduates and affiliated college staff in the broad fields of Biblical Studies, Christian Thought and History, and Practical Theology with Wipf and Stock Publishers of Eugene, Oregon. The ACT selects the best of its doctoral and research masters theses as well as monographs that offer the academic community, scholars, church leaders and the wider community uniquely Australian and New Zealand perspectives on significant research topics and topics of current debate. The ACT also provides opportunity for contributors beyond its graduates and affiliated college staff to publish monographs which support the mission and values of the ACT.

Rev Dr Graeme Chatfield
Series Editor and Associate Dean

Christ's Under-Shepherds

An Exploration of Pastoral Care Methods by
Elders in the Christian Reformed Churches of
Australia Relevant to the Circumstances
of Twenty-first-century Australia

LEO DOUMA

WIPF & STOCK · Eugene, Oregon

CHRIST'S UNDER SHEPHERDS
An Exploration of Pastoral Care Methods by Elders in the Christian Reformed Churches of Australia Relevant to the Circumstances of Twenty-first-century Australia

Copyright © 2016 Leo Douma. All rights reserved. Except for brief quotations in critical publications or reviews, no part of this book may be reproduced in any manner without prior written permission from the publisher. Write: Permissions, Wipf and Stock Publishers, 199 W. 8th Ave., Suite 3, Eugene, OR 97401.

Wipf & Stock
An Imprint of Wipf and Stock Publishers
199 W. 8th Ave., Suite 3
Eugene, OR 97401

www.wipfandstock.com

PAPERBACK ISBN: 978-1-4982-8091-4
HARDCOVER ISBN: 978-1-4982-8093-8

Manufactured in the U.S.A.

All Scripture quotations have been taken from the NIV.

Scripture taken from the HOLY BIBLE, NEW INTERNATIONAL VERSION. Copyright 1973, 1978, 1984 by International Bible Society. Used by permission of Zondervan Publishing House. All rights reserved.

Contents

Acknowledgments | vii
Glossary | xiii

1. Introduction | 1
2. Literature Search | 7
3. Methodology | 27
4. Analysis of the Focus Groups | 41
5. An Overview of the Action Research | 60
6. Conclusions | 91

Appendix | 103
Bibliography | 107

Acknowledgments

To the elders among you, I appeal as a fellow elder, a witness of Christ's sufferings and one who will also share in the glory to be revealed: be shepherds of God's flock that is under your care, serving as overseers—not because you must, but because you are willing, as God wants you to be; not greedy for money, but eager to serve; not lording it over those entrusted to you, but being examples of the flock. And when the Chief Shepherd appears, you will receive the crown of glory that will never fade away. (1 Peter 5:1–4)

THIS PUBLICATION HAS ITS beginnings in my desire as a pastor of over three decades to better equip the elders of the church to be worthy "under-shepherds" of the "Chief Shepherd," being examples to the flock that enables those they oversee to grow to become more like Jesus. This Doctor of Ministry project gave me the opportunity to explore the pastoral care methods used by elders in the Christian Reformed Churches of Australia and develop a process that assists elders to develop methods that are more relevant to the circumstances of twenty-first-century Australia. I do not claim that this research has now found the new way to do pastoral care. Rather it provides a practical process for elders in any church to develop a pastoral care method relevant to the situation in which they find themselves. We live in rapidly changing circumstances so such a process should be of real assistance to those charged to look after God's people.

I believe this book will be of value to pastors and elders of local congregations as well as those who are teaching at theological seminaries. This sentiment is shared by the Australian College of Theology (ACT), which has provided a grant for this doctoral project to be published. Its decision to select this work for their ACT Monograph Series was based on the responses of three eminent scholars who were appointed as examiners of the project, as noted in the ACT citation on conferring the Doctor of Ministry. This expert panel was convinced that the project had merit to be shared with a wider audience.

Dr Michael Milton, of the Reformed Theological Seminary in Charlotte, North Carolina, wrote in his assessment that

> Leo Douma has chosen a practical and compelling subject concerning pastoral care among Christian Reformed Churches in Australia and how his denomination can do a better job in the twenty-first century, postmodern context . . . [He] has shown the need for home visitation to realize greater discipleship goals for the pastoral effectiveness of the local leadership, but also chronicled the obstacles, both from the side of the clergy and elders and the people themselves. It was a very helpful discussion that should be considered by working pastors who are wrestling with the very issues Douma brings forth. . . . [He] has provided a very practical and helpful resource for working pastors. . . . His findings should be shared with others in the larger church. The problem he raises is a common one in many denominations and his research, reflections, and plans for correcting the problem should be shared with a broader audience. The church at large needs to learn from Douma's dissertation.

Dr Jeffrey Pugh, of the Melbourne School of Theology, wrote:

> This thesis is probably the first example of the Action Research approach to research within the context of ongoing ministry and could well serve as an exemplar to others of how this can be carried out for the benefit of the wider church; a wonderful example of the benefit of this form of qualitative research for the wider church. The methodological defence of this approach and the use of focus groups in the third chapter was first rate.

Dr Tim Witmer of Westminster Theological Seminary, Philadelphia, wrote as part of his assessment of the doctoral project:

> I am thrilled that Mr Douma has taken on this project. The flock in many congregations everywhere are being neglected by elders who are either too busy or who do not understand that shepherding is at the very heart of what they are to do as elders. . . . The author rightly notes the changes in the culture that made the practice [of home visiting by elders] increasingly difficult

including the busyness of all and the wide dispersion of people geographically rather than living in tightly knit community. . . . The research questions are excellent and get to the heart of the matter. They address comprehensive challenges that must be faced for elders, minister and members. . . . My summary conclusion is that Mr Douma has provided a great service to the Christian Reformed Church in not only providing the diagnosis of a crisis in pastoral care, but also taking steps toward a solution. . . . fascinating research which promises to benefit the flock of Jesus Christ as elders take more seriously their responsibility to be shepherds. Thank you for this thorough research and may the Lord bless its implementation.

I am deeply grateful to the ACT for this opportunity to have this work brought to a broader audience and pray that God will use it for the greater nurture of his people. My thanks goes to Dr Graeme Chatfield, Associate Dean and Director of Research at the ACT, for guiding me through the process with Wipf & Stock and also Rev. Chris Mulherin for copyediting and getting the thesis ready for publishing.

I also want to acknowledge those who assisted with the actual research of this project. Doctoral research is often an arduous solo effort by the researcher. But this research project would not have been possible without the contribution of many people who share my concern for the spiritual well-being of God's people and the capacity of those called as elders to oversee their spiritual well-being.

My gratitude is expressed to the many focus group participants, sixty-seven all together, who gave of their time, their openness and honesty, their insights and hunches, their joys and frustrations to give valuable data on the home visiting process in their churches. They are the church members and elders from the Christian Reformed Churches of Blacktown, St Marys, Wamberal, and Wollongong in New South Wales. My thanks also to the ministers of those churches who assisted with the organizing of the focus groups, my colleagues Reverends Colin Grant, Jack Kapinga, Nobin Shunmugam, and Werner Viljoen.

I am greatly indebted to the seven members of the action research team most of whom were involved for six months in team meetings, trialing ideas, observing what we planned and keeping diaries, reading numerous resources, and "doing the hard yards." They have provided the heart of this research with their humility, openness, and practical wisdom. They have provided deep insights as to what is needed for elders to truly represent their Lord Jesus to his people, to encourage them to grow in their faith. My thanks to Tony Deenick, Tony Eschler, Vance Green, Johan Grobler, Ray Hoekzema, Bill Meischke, and Paul Rees.

A special word is expressed for Bill Meischke who struggled with cancer during this time and who was taken to be with his Lord while I was editing the final draft of this research project. I was privileged to be asked to conduct Bill's funeral. He requested that I preach on Isaiah 6:8, "Here am I. Send me." Bill was a highly intelligent man who felt called to serve the church as an elder even though he was extremely busy in his capacity as an international economic consultant. While often being absent from team meetings Bill provided extensive diary notes outlining his thoughts, as well as insights gleaned from various books, websites, and other sources. Bill was typical of so many Reformed elders; very busy men who felt duty-bound to serve Christ in his church.

My appreciation is expressed for the eldership team I served with at the Christian Reformed Church of Sydney. It was in the ministry together with these brothers that I experienced pastoral ministry in reality with all its joys and sorrows, frustrations and satisfaction. Thank you for the time to research and write, for actually reading what I wrote, and interacting with it. Thank you for trusting me to train you over the years and forming a great working team. May you continue to develop and grow in the understanding of who and what you are in Jesus. May the way you do ministry together truly be representative of him who is the Great Shepherd!

My special thanks go to my doctoral supervisor, Dr John Reid, lecturer in Pastoral Care, retired from Morling College. We have come to see each other not only as supervisor and candidate but as colleagues and friends. John provided not only good insights and ideas on this research project but encouraged me to see my potential as a researcher and teacher. I also express sincere appreciation to Dr Graham Hill, lecturer in Pastoral Care at Morling College, who functioned as a secondary supervisor, reading this research project and guiding me through the system of preparing for submission.

I also express my appreciation for the assistance and use of the libraries at Morling College, Eastwood, NSW; Macquarie University, NSW; Reformed Theological College, Geelong, Victoria; and Calvin College, Grand Rapids, Michigan.

To my wife and best friend Elisabeth, thank you so much for your long-suffering patience as I was yet again in the study with the books, at the computer writing, to the neglect of the house and garden and time away together. Thank you for keeping me grounded and for selfless love that allows me to be involved in all my roles in ministry.

Above all else I express my deepest praise to my Lord and Saviour Jesus Christ. I am constantly moved at his grace, not only for allowing me to be a child of God, but also to be one of his representatives amongst his people, an under-shepherd of Christ. It is my prayer that this research assists in helping many other under-shepherds in their care of God's children, such that we all together sing the praises of King Jesus. As the Reformers said: Sola Deo gloria!

Leo Douma

Melbourne
Pentecost 2015

Glossary

GIVEN THAT READERS OF this research may consist of those not of a Christian Reformed Church background the following glossary of key terms is provided to assist in understanding when the terms are used in the body of this dissertation.

Christian Reformed Churches of Australia (CRCA): a conservative evangelical denomination established in Australia in 1951 by Dutch migrants with roots in the Gereformeerde Kerken in the Netherlands. The historical roots of the CRCA go back to the Reformation with John Calvin in Geneva together with his system of church governance and theology.

Elders: the ruling office in the local congregations of the CRCA. Elders are charged with the supervision of the local church. They are responsible for the spiritual well-being of all church members under their oversight. In the CRCA eldership is for male communicant members only. A distinction is made between elders who focus on preaching and teaching, also known as teaching elders or the minister, and elders who are charged with the supervision of the church, also know as ruling elders. Ministers are ordained for life. The elders, the "lay" leaders, are ordained for a three-year period, after which they are "retired" from office. After a period of a year or two they are eligible to be re-elected and then (again) installed to office.

Session: also known as the church council, the leadership team of a local congregation in the CRCA. Session consists of minister(s), elders, and deacons. None of these offices is higher or lower than the others, but each office has its own special task. All decisions for the local congregation, whether pastoral or administrative, come under the jurisdiction of the session and all decisions are made in collegiate. Session meets at least once per month.

Classis: a regional body made up of representatives from local church sessions; often seen as the state assembly of the CRCA. Classis is formed when convened by a local church session and is constituted by two representatives (usually a minister and elder) from each local church session. Classis meets every three months and deals with ecclesiastical matters of joint concern to the local sessions. The classis is seen as local church sessions covenanting together on issues of common concern and holding each other accountable.

Synod: the national assembly of the CRCA. It is formed when convened by a local church session and is constituted by four representatives (usually two ministers and two elders) from each classis. In the CRCA there are not higher church courts but broader assemblies. The local church session is the authority base in the CRCA.

Home visitation: the annual visitation of the families of church members in a local congregation by the elders. This visitation is written into the CRCA Church Order and is an "official" visit by two elders representing the session for the purpose of pastoral oversight and spiritual encouragement. It is the primary method of regular pastoral contact between the church members and the elders of the church.

Confessional standards: the CRCA has three confessions that define its teachings, namely the Belgic Confession, Heidelberg Catechism, and Canons of Dort. All elders at their ordination vow to uphold and defend these confessions. Any teaching or practice within the CRCA must conform to these standards.

I

Introduction

Introduction

THE IMPETUS FOR THIS research project stems from the fact that the researcher is an ordained minister of the Christian Reformed Churches of Australia (CRCA). As such the researcher has been working very closely with the local church elders for over thirty years in three congregations.

CRCA Church Governance

In the Christian Reformed Churches' governance the ruling authority lies with the elders who, together with the minister, form the Session or Church Council. There is no higher authority in the CRCA than the elders. The Classis and Synod are broader assemblies with delegated authority from the local church councils.

It is the eldership that determines the direction of the CRCA. All decisions at the local church council are made in collegiate, that is, the minister cannot of his own accord determine church policy or make decisions about pastoral matters. The Church Order of the CRCA makes it clear that the pastoral care of the congregation rests not with the minister only but with all the elders. In the Reformed system the elders, as the pastoral carers of the church members, oversee the church members' life and doctrine.

Pastoral Care by Home Visitation

The traditional manner in which this oversight or pastoral care has been carried out is by means of an annual home visit. This consists of two elders visiting a family for an evening and together with devotions and prayer discussing with the parents and children their personal relationship with God, as well as other matters that relate to that family. It is also an opportunity for the family to discuss with the elders matters in regard to the life of the church.

From the above it can be seen that the elders play a vital role in the life of a CRCA congregation. They are not just a governing board. The elders are the primary pastoral carers who set the spiritual direction and tone of the congregation and determine its goals.

Training Provided

To assist the elders in their vital work in the congregation the researcher has been providing training for elders for the past decade. The researcher also initiated training at the Classis level designed for elders to consider issues in relation to new directions for the churches.

This training was provided because it was found that the elders had previously been "thrown in the deep end," called to the responsible task of leading and pastoring the congregation with limited knowledge and skills.

Problems With Elders' Pastoral Care

Even though training has been provided, there are ongoing concerns about the functioning of the eldership. The system of care provided by the elders, namely the annual home visitation, is unable to function as it should due to major changes in the circumstances of the elders and church members.

Personal observation by the researcher has made it clear that over the past decade there has been a steady decline in the number of elders who actually provide pastoral care by means of the annual visitation, to the extent that it is now virtually non-existent in the researcher's own congregation.

Work and Time Pressure

One reason identified for the lack of home visitation has been the work rate of the elders in their day jobs. A recent government survey made clear the impact of the demanding work hours for most workers today.[1] The length of the hours and the pressure of the work means that elders find themselves exhausted and unable to do much in their role as elders except for the barest minimum of attending Session meetings and some forward planning.

This concern regarding time and lack of visitation is not an isolated incident with the researcher's local elders. Recent writings in other local church bulletins and the CRCA seminary magazine indicate similar concerns about the failure of elders to provide the traditional home visits.[2]

Elders' Suitability

Even if annual visits were to be made, there are doubts as to the elders' suitability to provide the pastoral care that is required in our current postmodern setting. Anecdotal evidence, such as the bits of conversation heard at recent ministers' conferences, have raised questions about the pastoral care provided by elders. One minister asked, in frustration, "what do we do with elders?" Another referred to the method of home visiting as "patriarchal" or "policing."

Value of the Process

Congregational members, who do still from time to time receive a home visit by the elders, wonder about the value of the process. There is a growing tendency for the younger generation to prefer not to be visited, some having suggested they see the process as intrusive and irrelevant.

Lack of Community

It is becoming clear that an aspect of what creates difficulty for the system of home visitation is that the sense of community that underpinned church life in sixteenth-century Europe no longer exists for many CRCA congregations in twenty-first-century Australia. When the pastoral system was designed, the church members lived in towns and villages and the elders saw most of the church members constantly throughout the week. The first draft of a Church Order even called on elders to visit families weekly. Recent discussions with an elder from South Africa revealed that all the families in his pastoral district lived in the same street as he did. So the annual home visits

---

1. Relationships Forum, *An Unexpected Tragedy*.
2. E.g., Esselbrugge, *BRC Church Bulletin*. And Capill, *RTC Monthly*, 20.

were built upon frequent social contacts, where people knew each other well. In the current Australian setting the membership in many CRCA congregations is thinly spread out amongst numerous suburbs. The various church families and their elders have little contact except for the few moments after a church service. Elders making an annual home visit often do so with families that do not know the elders personally. Any revised approach to pastoral care will need to factor in this lack of community.

Reactive/Proactive Pastoral Care

A further factor for consideration is that much of the pastoral care that is provided by the minister and elders in the CRCA can be called reactive pastoral care. The CRCA Church Order refers to "the sick, the distressed, the aged and the erring."[3] While it is agreed that support for church members in need is a very important part of the care that is to be provided, it is argued that this is only part of the picture. What is also important is what could be called proactive pastoral care. That is, spending time with church members so that they are spiritually nurtured, discipled, and trained. This is more in line with Ephesians 4 where Paul advocates that the "pastor-teachers" are to "equip the saints for ministry."

CRCA Synod Vision

This emphasis on the need for a proactive approach to pastoral care can be seen in the recent decision of the CRCA Synod. At its 2006 meeting the synod adopted a four-fold vision statement. Under the banner of "a church reforming to reach the lost for Christ," it was decided that the CRCA congregations needed to work on four areas. Involved in these key areas is the need for spiritual formation to maturity, discipling and training, as well as the need to reconsider the churches' way of doing their ministry.[4]

The Research Question

The general aim of this proposed research project is to review the above concerns and develop a strategy that will provide a practicable method for

---

3. Christian Reformed Churches of Australia, *Church Order*, 26.
4. Christian Reformed Churches of Australia, *Acts 2006*, I-14–I-26.

the current situation of the CRCA elders, as well as that of the church members, including a proactive approach to pastoral care. The research question is:

> What kind of pastoral care, provided by the elders in the CRCA:
>
> > is actually practicable by the elders
> >
> > > *given their ever-increasing working hours and employment demands*
> > >
> > > *given their lay/voluntary capacity*
> > >
> > > *given their limited training, due to lack of time and resources, in the skills of pastoral care*
> >
> > will be received by the church members
> >
> > > *given the cultural changes that show a tendency in some quarters to see the current method of pastoral care as patriarchal and intrusive*
> > >
> > > *given the lack of community that was assumed under the current method of pastoral care*
> > >
> > > *given the limited amount of time church members allow for pastoral visitation due to work and family demands*
> >
> > will be proactive rather than only reactive pastoral care
> >
> > > *providing for ways to help church members care for each other*
> > >
> > > *providing for members to grow spiritually*
> > >
> > > *providing for members to be equipped for service*
> > >
> > > *providing for members to disciple others*

Methodology

The method used to answer the research question is that of action research (AR). This is the preferred method of the Australian College of Theology for Doctor of Ministry research projects. This method is very suited to this particular research in that the AR process is designed to assist participants to improve their own work or ministry practices in their own context. The role of the researcher in AR is that of a facilitator or coach. In other words, this research assisted elders to find their own solution to the concerns about the pastoral care provided by elders in the CRCA. This research is thus not a theological dissertation, nor a New Testament biblical study, or even a

Church Order review. It is a review of ministry practice. That is the nature of a Doctor of Ministry project.

Chapter Outlines

In chapter 2 of this research dissertation a literature search is provided which outlines the history, biblical basis, purpose, and benefits of home visitation by the elders. It also outlines the changes in culture that are now causing problems with the system and also practical issues of concern. The latter provides support for the suppositions in this introduction, which had been gleaned from anecdotal evidence. What is surprising is that the numerous concerns mentioned already date back to the 1960s, the early days of the establishment of the CRCA, and prior to that in the Netherlands and United States.

Chapter 3 delineates the methodology used in conducting this research. Focus groups were used to establish objectively the current state of home visiting by elders and how they have been received by the church members. Questions about a possible revised approach to pastoral care by the elders were also raised. This chapter also explains the AR process and how the results can be seen as plausible and valid as qualitative research.

Chapter 4 provides a summary of the results of the focus groups. This is based on the verbatim transcripts of eight focus groups. This analysis confirmed the concerns that were raised in this introduction and the literature search. What is surprising is the extent and depth of the concerns expressed by both the congregational members and the elders, given that the majority of the focus group participants were older, long-term members of the congregations. What further confirms these results is the data from the international comparison.

Chapter 5 provides a summary narrative of the AR process by seven elders. This summary is based on the verbatim record of seven team meetings with these elders, together with their diary notes and other resources. The key results show that the elders focused on providing oversight, example, and discipling by means of small groups to compensate for lack of community, time, and relationships.

Chapter 6 outlines the conclusions of the research and the recommendations in terms of a revised approach to pastoral care by the CRCA elders. It also suggests training requirements for elders and ministers in the CRCA if the suggested approach by the AR team is to function well.

2

Literature Search

Introduction

IN THE CHRISTIAN REFORMED Churches of Australia (CRCA) pastoral care of the church members is a primary function of the elders. The ordination liturgy for elders states that: "*elders are responsible for the spiritual wellbeing of all members* under their supervision. For this reason the elders shall *faithfully visit the members* of the church and discuss with them the privileges and responsibilities of serving Christ."[1]

The Church Order of the CRCA states: "With the ministers of the church the elders shall: a. be examples to the congregations in all things; b. oversee the doctrine and life of the members of the congregation . . . c. *faithfully provide pastoral care* for the congregation."[2]

In terms of the pastoral care to be provided the Church Order says: "As shepherds of the flock, the minister and *elders shall visit all members* and regular attenders, as a rule at *least once a year*, to encourage them to live by faith, comfort them in adversity, and warn them against errors in doctrine and life."[3]

---

1. Reformed Churches of Australia, *Book of Forms*, 252.
2. Christian Reformed Church of Australia, *Church Order*, 14.
3. Ibid., 26.

Historical Background

The history of the CRCA Church Order extends from the time of the Reformation.

Calvin

The principles of the Reformed Church polity were first enunciated by John Calvin in his *Ordonnances Ecclésiastiques*. These church ordinances were developed by Calvin in Geneva in the mid 1500s. Central to his ordinances were the elders who were laymen and seen as "the most characteristic of Calvin's institutions"[4] even "the heart of Calvin's system"[5] and were responsible for church discipline. The elders were chosen for their "good character and spiritual wisdom. They were to watch over the lives of all, to admonish lovingly the disorderly, and where necessary, to report to their brethren in the Consistory, who would take measures for the fraternal correction of the offenders."[6]

Calvin states: "The first foundation of discipline is to provide a place for private admonition; that is, if anyone does not perform his duty willingly, or behaves insolently, or does not live honorably . . . he should allow himself to be admonished . . . Let pastors and presbyters be especially watchful to do this, for their duty is not only to preach to the people, but to warn and exhort in every house."[7]

Reformed Churches

What Calvin advocated and prescribed in his *Ordinances* was taken up by the Reformed Churches of the Netherlands. At their very first formal gathering, the Convention of Wezel in 1568, the following article was adopted with respect to elders, which is quoted in full:

> No doubt [the elders'] office demands that each diligently keep watch over his own parish or district, and visit the members under their care from house to house at least once per week, and furthermore as often as is the custom according to the regulation of each church. This shall be done especially close

---

4. Chadwick, *The Reformation*, 84.
5. Walker, *History of the Christian Church*, 354.
6. McNeill, *The History and Character of Calvinism*, 163.
7. Calvin, *Institutes*, 1230.

to the time of the celebration of the Lord's Supper. They shall faithfully investigate whether they (the church members) manifest themselves uprightly in walk and conduct, in the duties of godliness, in the faithful instruction of their households in the matter of family prayers, morning and evening prayers, and such like matters; they shall admonish them to steadfastness, or strengthen them to patience, or spur them on to a serious-minded fear of God; such as need comfort and admonition, and if need be they shall report such a matter to their fellow elders, who together with them are appointed to exercise discipline; and besides these matters they shall correct that which can be corrected, according to the gravity of the sin committed; nor shall they neglect, each one in his district, to encourage them to send their children to catechism.[8]

The above article, while being very instructive was deemed to be too long and so eighteen years later the Synod of Gravenhage in 1586 stated that the elders should "conduct family visiting for the edification of the congregation . . . especially in order to comfort the members of the congregation, to teach and also exhort others to profess the Christian religion."[9] This article was later adopted by the Synod of Dort (1618–1619) whose Church Order was definitive for Reformed Churches for centuries, and forms the basis for the current CRCA Church Order.

Historic Conditions

Reviewing the article from the Synod of Wezel it can be seen that it called for weekly visitations by the elders. In 1586 the Synod of Gravenhage, in its summary statement, stipulated that elders visit the church members "both before and after the Lord's Supper, as time and circumstances may require."[10]

The frequency of visitation by the elders reflects the historic circumstances of the time. It has been argued that the weekly visitations replaced the Roman Catholic practice of confession. The need to educate church members of the Reformed understanding of the Lord's Supper, as distinct from the Roman Catholic mass, made it necessary for the elders to personally talk to the members of the congregation concerning the significance of

---

8. Cf. Cammenga, "Family Visitation." Also De Ridder, *In His Service—Family Visitation*, 7. Hoeksema, "Family Visitation," 27–28. Swart, "The Proper Manner of Conducting Family Visitation."

9. De Ridder, *In His Service—Family Visitation*, 8.

10. Swart, "The Proper Manner of Conducting Family Visitation," 2.

the Lord's Supper and the spiritual attitude with which they should come. Having witnessed the corruption of a merely formalistic approach there was a keenly felt need to promote true spirituality.[11] So the frequency of home visits reflected the fact that the Reformed Churches in the Netherlands were in their infancy and it was necessary to provide church members with more careful supervision and instruction in the faith.[12]

Hoeksema argues that the family visitation was not a "replacement or substitution for the Roman Catholic confessions but actually going back to the practice of the early church fathers and what was taught in the New Testament."[13] De Jong notes that the writings of Clement of Alexander and Cyprian demonstrate that members were visited in their homes: "It is evident that the first fathers of the churches did not deem the public instruction given in the church at the time of worship was sufficient to meet the demands of spiritual life. They sought to supplement the preaching with a type of spiritual care in which the members were contacted in their homes."[14]

Biblical Basis

Cammenga, like other Reformed writers[15] admits, "There is no specific text of scripture that mandates annual home visitation. Family visitation is rather implied in those passages of Scripture that call the elders to watch over the souls of the people of God, the sheep as well as the lambs."[16]

The key biblical arguments put forward by the Reformed writers for home visiting by the elders can be summarized as follows:

Old Testament

In the Old Testament the elders were the magistrates or rulers among the people of God. They were men of experience, wisdom, dignity, and

---

11. Ibid.

12. Hanko, *Notes on the Church Order*, 108–109. Decker, "The Elders and Family Visitation."

13. Hoeksema, "Family Visitation," 28.

14. De Jong, "Taking Heed to the Flock," 40. See also Van Dam, *The Elder*, 163.

15. Hoeksema, "Family Visitation," 28–29. De Jong, "The Scriptural Basis of Family Visitation," 62. Larson, "A Reformed Perspective of Home Visitation," 38. Van Brussel, "Elders Conference in Victoria," 7.

16. Cammenga, "Family Visitation," 1.

authority.[17] This was most clearly established in Numbers 11 where God told Moses that his task of ruling the people was to be shared by seventy elders. So the elders were the overseers of the people with Moses.[18]

New Testament

In the New Testament the elders were members of the Sanhedrin, the main ruling body of the Jews. The synagogue with its body of elders became the pattern for the local churches. In the Jerusalem church it was the accepted practice that there was a ruling office. When Paul and Barnabas worked among the Jews it was their custom to appoint elders before they moved on.[19]

Under Shepherds

The elders are seen as "ruling" in the place of Jesus Christ. As one writer put it:

> To understand the Reformed view of elders there is no job description or mandate given by the Apostles. We have to study the whole Bible to see how the Lord Jesus, the Great Shepherd cares for the sheep of his flock, and how he appointed people to continue this pastoral care for him. Christ Himself did not only proclaim the Good News to the crowds or congregation; he paid special attention to the specific needs of individuals.[20]

The church is seen as being established and maintained by Christ himself through his Holy Spirit. The Heidelberg Catechism states: "I believe that the Son of God, through his Word and Spirit . . . gathers, protects and preserves for himself a community chosen for eternal life and united in true faith."[21]

For the members of the church to attain to spiritual maturity, Christ has given offices (Ephesians 4:11) and they are the means by which Christ provides his care and oversight. Elders are thus regarded as called by the Lord and have his authority to work in the church, being under shepherds

---

17 Van Brussel, "The Elder's Office in Scripture and History," 7. See also Vanderwell, *Now That You are an Elder*, 5–6.

18. De Graaf, "What is an Elder, Studies in the Pastoral Letters (1)," 3.

19. Van Brussel, "The Elder's Office in Scripture and History," 8.

20. Hoving, "The Elder as Pastor; Home Visits," 23.

21. CRCA, *Book of Forms*, 82.

of the great shepherd (1 Pet 5:1–4). Therefore, the church members must submit themselves to the elders (1 Thess 5:12–14; Heb 13:17).[22]

When elders encourage, challenge, or comfort the members of the church under their care, it's not their own ideas or insights they put forward. "To give biblical leadership as an elder is to let the sheep hear the voice of the Good Shepherd. The elder's own opinion about the issue at hand is unimportant. What is crucial is that as office bearers, elders speak according to the mind of Christ."[23] (Cf. John 10:4)

Key Text

The Bible passage that most hints at home visitation by the elders and is the most quoted by Reformed writers to provide a scriptural basis for the practice is Acts 20:17–38. Williamson writes:

> Paul sets before all of these Ephesian elders his own ministry as a model for them. He exhorts all of them to "pay careful attention . . . to all the flock, in which the Holy Spirit has made you overseers." (Acts 20:28) "You yourselves know," he reminds them, "how I lived among you the whole time from the first day . . . how I did not shrink from declaring to you anything that was profitable, and teaching you in public and from house to house . . . [and] for three years I did not cease night or day to admonish everyone with tears." (Acts 20:18, 20, 31) And then he adds these telling words: "I have shown you in every way, laboring like this, that you must support the weak."[24]

The Purpose of Home Visitation

Sittema writes, "The only way an elder can keep his bearings is to keep his mind on the assigned purpose. Why must he do this work?"[25] De Jong provides an answer to that by stating clearly, "The first conscious aim of

---

22. De Jong, "The Scriptural Basis of Family Visitation," 60–61. See also Van Brussel, "Elders Conference in Victoria," 6.

23. Van Dam, *The Elder*, 152.

24. Williamson, "The Importance of Home Visitation." See also Larson, "A Reformed Perspective of Home Visitation," 38. Hoving, "The Elder as Pastor; Home Visits," 24. Hoeksema, "Family Visitation," 29.

25. Sittema, "Pastoring With a Purpose," 14.

Reformed family visitation is the development of the spiritual life of the individual."[26]

So the purpose of an official home visit is to measure the spiritual health of the members being visited.[27] In the Reformed tradition it has been a significant tool for spiritual direction.[28]

Accountability

Faith is not just an assent to biblical knowledge but involves a personal relationship with the Lord. As is experienced by all Christians that walk is not always consistent but involves times when individuals drift away from God. There is thus a real need to hold each other accountable. It is granted that it is the work of the Holy Spirit to change the hearts of those needing to come closer again to God, but the Spirit uses human means.[29] "Family visitation is the exercise of the pastoral office of the elders carried on systematically in such a way as to encourage the members in sanctified living, to strengthen weaknesses in their lives, to admonish members regarding shortcomings in their Christian walk, and to strengthen the church by these means."[30]

Resources

In helping church members experience spiritual formation in their lives there is a need for the elders to use the tools for spiritual formation that are provided by the church, such as those found in the confessions. From that foundation and perspective the elders can encourage the church members to be disciplined and nurture their own spiritual development through such things as reading the Bible, meditating on Scripture, praying alone and together, participating in retreats and so forth.[31]

---

26. De Jong, "The Spiritual Purpose of Family Visitation," 21.
27. Vanderpyl, "Elder to Elder," 34.
28. De Koning, *Guiding the Faith Journey*, 59.
29. De Jong, "The Spiritual Purpose of Family Visitation," 21.
30. Wesseling, "What is an Elder to do?" 18.
31. Tamminga, *A Handbook for Elders*, 38–39. Also Tamminga, *The Elder's Handbook*, 47–48.

Covenant Community

The elders need to help the congregation to see that their spiritual life has two dimensions: love for God and love for each other. The Reformed approach to spirituality is covenantal: "I will be your God and you will be my people." (Exod 6:7) So there is a need to inspire the personal relationship each member has with God, but also their relationship with each other. Being covenant minded, the elders are to assist in establishing people in God and establishing the people in community.[32]

The way the church members interact with each other is part of and affects their spiritual development. The Apostle Paul teaches that "the body grows and builds itself up in love as each part does its work." (Eph 4:16) True spiritual community is seen in the way the members care for each other and demonstrate Christ's love to each other. The most fundamental pastoral care is that done by the church members for each other as they mutually encourage each other and hold each other accountable.[33]

Equipping for Service

The purpose of home visitation also includes equipping the church members for service. Ephesians 4 clearly outlines the task of the elders: "[Christ] gave some to be . . . pastors and teachers to prepare God's people for works of service, so that the body of Christ may be built up until we all . . . become mature." (Eph 4:11–13) Sittema comments: "The purpose of an elder is never only to deal with an immediate problem, to come down hard on a specific sin, to lend a listening ear during a difficult time. The purpose is always greater than the immediate. It always includes the call to stimulate, encourage, or restore the brother or sister to positive and active service in his or her life!"[34]

---

32. Tamminga, *A Handbook for Elders*, 36–37. Also Tamminga, *The Elder's Handbook*, 44–45.

33. Tamminga, *A Handbook for Elders*, 36–37. And Tamminga, *The Elder's Handbook*, 44–45. See also Berghoef, and De Koster, *The Elders Handbook, A Practical Guide*, 91: "Family visiting draws the church together into the local communion of saints—a communion all seek." Van Brussel, "Pastoral Care by Elders," 19.

34. Sittema, "Pastoring with a Purpose," 15–16.

Visiting at Home

De Koning argues that home visiting "remains a helpful strategy" in building the spiritual health of a congregation because families are the basic unit of society and what happens in the home is of critical importance to the lives of those church members and thus to the spiritual welfare of the congregation. In the home the elders can see the dynamics of the family that give shape to the faith journey of the family members.[35]

However, De Koning concedes, "the home visit is not the only strategy for developing spirituality within the congregation. Yet the connection between the spirituality of the home and the spirituality of the congregation is significant. To enter homes with a focus on the spirituality allows leaders to have a positive effect on the congregation's life with God."[36]

Personal Contact

De Jong argues that if the work of spiritual formation is to be: "carried out effectively, the elders must know the spiritual conditions and needs of the flock over which they have been placed. How can this ever be done, unless there is some form of intimate contact between the officers and members of the church?"[37] Concerned that the elders must give an account to God for their oversight of the flock he goes on to say: "Until it is proven that there exists some better form of supervision than that of family visitation we do well not only to safeguard this institution for future generations by faithfully discharging it but also to improve it constantly by studying and discussing its nature and methods."[38]

Being Examples

A further reason for elders having close and regular contact with the church members is demonstrated by Van Dam who says:

> A most powerful way of teaching the gospel message and its implications for knowing God in a life of communion with him is by example . . . The elders are to be a living embodiment of the gospel . . . When an office bearer exemplifies and teaches the

---

35. De Koning, *Guiding the Faith Journey*, 60.
36. Ibid., 63. Also see Hoeksema, "Family Visitation," 34–35.
37. De Jong, "The Necessity of Family Visitation," 40.
38. Ibid.

gospel message and how it impacts life, he works for the salvation of those who listen to him. "Watch your life and doctrine closely. Persevere in them, because if you do, you will save both yourself and your hearers." (1 Tim 4:16)[39]

The Benefits of Church Visitation

The benefits of home visitation, giving further detail to the general purpose of spiritual growth, can be summarized as follows:

> Elder visits manifest personal care in a way that binds people to the church.
>
> Elder visits inform the elders of the spiritual state of the congregation and are a way of checking the spiritual pulse of the congregation.
>
> They build capital in people's lives so that if elders need to confront problems there is a relational context.
>
> Visits afford the opportunity to remove misconceptions and misunderstandings otherwise unknown to the elders.
>
> It displays to the membership that elders are taking their spiritual responsibilities seriously, and it therefore serves as an exhortation by example that each part of the body of Christ is expected to be faithful.
>
> It demonstrates the parity between the [pastor] and the elders and shows people that the pastors are not the only ones they should seek out for counsel.
>
> It allows members to express concerns directly to the leadership. Included in this is the ability to receive feedback on the pastor's ministry from people who would be uncomfortable in talking directly to him.
>
> Families see pastoral care modeled in their own home.
>
> Elders can preempt members who are tempted to make a bad decision or to complicate a difficult situation in some way.[40]

---

39. Van Dam, *The Elder*, 150.

40. Unknown, "Eighteen Reasons for Elders to do Home Visitation," 92. See also De Jong, "The Value of Family Visitation," 18–22. Fennema, "On Doing Home Visitation," 32–33. Vander Pyl, *Church Order Commentary*, 3–74.

The Problems with Home Visitation

The purpose and benefits of home visits as noted above indicate there is a biblical validity and pastoral value for the elders to maintain the practice. But a review of past and recent literature makes it clear that in practical terms in the current setting serious concerns are being expressed across various continents.

A Dutch elder writes: "Without any doubt or contradiction, after many years of experience with pastoral visits in various congregations, one can say that pastoral visits are in a crisis."[41]

One minister demonstrates this crisis on his blog. He is quoted in full to demonstrate his confusion and despair:

> Please enlighten me. Although I'm not exactly a goal-orientated person, one of my goals this year is to help my elders and deacons embrace the calling of their offices more fully. One of the difficult things about that is the role of elders. Here is the dilemma: Elders, in the Reformed tradition, are responsible for the oversight and spiritual welfare of all members of the congregation. Often throughout history, that has been accomplished (or presumed accomplished) through the annual house visitations. The problem is, I've discerned two very distinct groups in our church: 1) People who believe elders (and, of course, the minister) *ought* to visit every home every year and are offended that we do not currently do that, and 2) people who believe elders (and, of course, the minister) *ought not to* do home visits unless invited and are offended at the idea that we would invite ourselves over. Both groups, not surprisingly, are age-defined. The former *generally* includes the older people in my congregation and the latter *generally* includes the younger. (There are, of course, exceptions.) I am not convinced that the time-honored *Huis Bezoek* is actually effective, nor am I convinced that it isn't. Surely the biggest problem is to convince elders to actually *care* about the members of the congregation and convince the congregation that the elders actually *do* care about them. What do you think? Should elders (and possibly, the minister) do annual visitations? Is it effective? Should we do them *only* upon invitation? Is it necessary? Is it appropriate? Is it rude? How do you provide for the oversight and care of the members in your congregation. Please let me know![42]

---

41. Askes, *The Elder in a Troublesome Time for the Church*, 19.
42. Ten Clay, *Comments on: Elders & Huis Bezoek*.

Two Australian ministers are definite that change is needed. One, a theological lecturer writes:

> Increasingly Reformed Churches are having to ask hard questions about our traditional model of eldership . . . an increasing number of people do not find an annual home visit very adequate as an expression of pastoral care and they are not about to open spiritually to someone they barely know. And the men in eldership are often crazily busy. Many work long hours and have families caught up in the frenzy of twenty-first-century living. They find it hard to make their time stretch to eldership alongside everything else. Very often not even the annual home visit is being done. What do we do? It seems foolish to just ask everyone to pedal harder. Something needs to change.[43]

In a similar vein a senior CRCA minister states:

> Today's eldership is in crisis . . . The problem is if we "drop the bar" and abandon elder's home visits, we seem to be relinquishing something that at least indicated the high value of pastoral care. On the other hand, how can we continue with an ineffective approach, where elders don't have the time or even the likelihood of making improvements that will deliver a more responsible pastoral care to people?[44]

It needs to be admitted that there have always been concerns to ensure home visits by elders are done well. But the current increase in failure of traditional pastoral care has much to do with changes in culture. One commentator says, "I believe that fulfilling [the task of pastoral care] is more difficult than has been the case for centuries."[45]

There have been massive changes in the past fifty years and the majority of that in the last fifteen years with the development of the personal computer.[46] People think differently now than fifty years ago. They are no longer committed to institutions and they are suspicious of authority figures.[47] Instead of looking to the church for their spiritual nurture many now view the church with fear and suspicion.

---

43. Capill, "Ministry Spot," 20.
44. Groenenboom, "Pastoral Care in the Community."
45. Goodliff, *Care in a Confused Climate*, 5.
46. Sittema, "Pastoring with a Purpose," 3–4.
47. Capill, "Ministry Spot," 23.

Instead of seeing the church as God's family, the heart of their social and religious life, there is now a consumer mentality towards the church.[48] There is no longer any "brand loyalty" to a congregation or denomination. Many attend several churches depending on the styles of worship, teaching, or programs they are looking for. While the postmoderns highly value relationships they don't value commitment.[49] "The concept of 'church membership' that has served for nearly two millennia to give visible testimony to spiritual commitment and communal 'belongingness' has gone the way of the dinosaur."[50]

Practical Issues of Concern

Searching through the literature the following list of practical concerns can be identified in regards to the elders conducting home visitations:

Time

Elders are struggling to find the time to conduct their pastoral care program well. One minister writes: "There is a crisis of resources: elders are struggling to do what they are expected to do. The main issue is time: busy people feel they have huge stresses on their schedules, families suffer, and a sense of failure intensifies it all."[51]

In addition to the remarks in the Australian context comments from an American minister indicate similar things in regards to the elders' time: "The number of families varies a bit, but an elder calls on around twenty-five families . . . but all of the elders sit on at least one of the church committees as a liaison. In addition, all are involved with choir or other church activities such as household Bible study groups, or teaching catechism . . . I am always conscious of the tensions that are present in these comments."[52]

Not only do the elders have trouble with time for home visitation, but so also do many families that are to be visited. As an example, one minister writes: "In our modern world visitation seems so difficult because of the deranged schedules most of our members have: soccer for the children,

---

48. Ibid.
49. Ibid.
50. Sittema, "Pastoring with a Purpose," 5.
51. Groenenboom, "Pastoral Care in the Community." See also Esselbrugge, *From the Manse*.
52. De Koning, "Home Visit."

parent-teacher meetings, business obligations. Modern schedules seem to render home visits an impossibility and an imposition."[53]

Unprepared

Numerous articles indicate that many men feel unprepared and inadequate for their role as elders. They doubt if they have what it takes to be a spiritual guide[54] and can feel quite overwhelmed.[55] Typical of the articles is: "There is a crisis of confidence . . . elders often doubt whether they have what it takes to address the typical raft of pastoral issues and concerns."[56] Says another: "Very few churches have a program of preparation in which people are enrolled prior to their call to be an elder; which means most elders start the work of eldership feeling unprepared for the challenge of the work."[57]

Effectiveness

Numerous articles also raise questions as to the effectiveness of home visiting by elders. As one Australian minister expresses it: "There is a crisis of effectiveness. Is it realistic or responsible to expect an annual visit to address the pastoral needs of any person? The annual visit is just not working. This is not a matter of 'fault'; it is a matter of changing culture. People tend to only open up with others when there is a pre-existent relationship. It is unrealistic to expect elders to have such a high level of relationship with anywhere from fifteen to twenty families in a typical elder's district."[58]

In an American blog we read: "Home visits have been a struggle in many churches. It has been a perennial source of frustration as long as I have been in the ministry. When done well, it has been a source of great blessing. However, between the limitations of time, flimsy relationships between elders and members, and poor conversations at visits the home visits have suffered."[59]

---

53. Hughes, "In the Church—Visit and Prosper." See also ibid.
54. De Koning, "Do I Have What It Takes?"
55. De Koning, "Getting Started as a First-Time Elder."
56. Groenenboom, "Pastoral Care in the Community."
57. De Koning, "Just-in-Time Learning." See also Hanko, "The Calling of Elders."
58. Groenenboom, "Pastoral Care in the Community." See also De Koning, "Home Visit."
59. De Koning, "Elders and Spiritual Formation."

The question about effectiveness is not just a recent one. In the 1960s an Australian minister wrote: "It is the experience of most of our elders that so frequently our visits are not nearly as effective as we would like them to be. There is no real discussion; the talk remains a monologue. What is the reason, and what can we do to prevent this unpleasant experience, and the sense of frustration that comes after it?"[60]

Loss of Authority

Another concern raised by several writers relates to the perceived authority of the elders. An elder writes in a blog: "I have served as an elder . . . and have been involved with many home visits. My observation is that responses to these visits are by and large contrived, failing to glean from the visits true and heartfelt dialogue on the most important subjects that affect the respondents' relationship with Christ . . . Somewhere along the line elders . . . have lost their authority over congregations, making many attempts to nurture ineffectual."[61]

While the above comments are recent and from the United States, already in the early 1960s concerns were being expressed in Australia and New Zealand. For example a senior minister wrote: "I am afraid to say that B's diagnosis to a great extent is correct. That the picture of our church life often is more deformed than reformed and that our members who are to nominate candidates for eldership sometimes don't have the faintest idea of what is expected from an office-bearer of Christ, and that in the offices we lack the real gifts of sanctified and full-grown personalities, yes, let me call it: it is the man of God we need."[62]

Unwilling Church Members

Two American ministers already noted in the early 1990s that there were those who were unwilling to have home visits. Says De Jong: "Some would claim [church members] do not like family visitation at all; they tolerate it simply because it has been the rule for so many years and the consistory still insists on it. If the members of the congregation were permitted to decide

---

60. Van Brussel, "Pastoral Care by Elders," 23.
61. De Koning, "Home Visit."
62 Vander Bom, "The Man of God," 4. See also Vander Pyl "Talks From an Elder to Elders: The Elder Through Many Eyes," 15. Van Brussel, "Pastoral Care by Elders," 22.

on the matter, the vote in favor of its abolishment would be overwhelming . . . the members are unwilling or unable to discuss spiritual matters."[63]

Cammenga writes: "Another threat to family visitation is a lack of cooperation on the part of the family being visited. At times it happens that the family resents really the presence of the minister and elders and views family visitation as an unwelcome intrusion into their personal lives."[64]

Lack of Confidentiality

A CRCA elder in the mid 1960s wrote of his concern about elders keeping confidential what they were told on home visits: "How many elders can be trusted with a confidential matter? How many discuss home visitations and contributions with their wives, family or friends?"[65]

Annual Visit Not Enough

There is an ongoing expression of concern that the annual home visit by the elders is quite simply inadequate to achieve the purpose of their pastoral care. This is not new. For example a CRCA minister wrote in 1964: "Several times I have stressed the point that one home visit; one talk a year cannot possibly do, to build up a good relationship. How can you come close to each other, how can you understand each other when you try to see something of a man's inner life just once a year? . . . I want to stress the idea of an elder as a regular visitor, a kind of family friend in a small part of the congregation."[66]

In the same year a New Zealand elder reminisced about his experience of home visiting when he was a child:

> A clear example of this is my home church and family back in Holland. There one would see the elders once a year for one hour and no more. From what I can remember about those conversations is that they were very stiff and formal with very little spiritual value. I suppose they would report back to the session . . . that the conversation was stiff and that the spiritual level was low. They would probably report further that the boys were not present or that the boys never said a word. The tragedy about

---

63. De Jong, "Objections to Family Visitation," 89.
64. Cammenga, "Family Visitation (2)." See also Webb, "On Pastoral Visitation."
65. Achterstraat, "She Won't Say Nothing."
66. De Ruiter, "The Elder and Young Folk," 13. See also De Ruiter, "The Elder and His Work," 10.

this is that they did not see that they themselves were to blame for most of this bad report. They never—no never—had a heart to heart conversation with either Mum or Dad. We as boys did not even know who our elder was, and the only time we found out was the time they came to ask for a donation. How tragic. Are we going in the same direction? I think we are heading that way. Most elders may give a visit once a year but it would be more like every one and half years. No I am convinced that the elder fails to do his God given task in overseeing the flock allotted to him if he does not have more contact than this. He should *know* his sheep, know them spiritually; know their weaknesses. He should make so many contacts, until he knows them.[67]

Not Relating to Youth

One CRCA minister wrote, again, back in the mid-sixties:

> One of the features of our time is the devaluation of the offices of authority and discipline; young people don't accept your advice and warnings just because of your office; you have to prove your value as an office bearer and otherwise you have lost it. . . . "Worthless," was the opinion of a young bloke, after a home visit, "Completely worthless; oh sorry, I hope you won't be angry about it, but they did not understand a bit of it; I think he meant well, but he just didn't listen. They did not understand me."[68]

Becomes a Formality

With the home visits by elders being "official," and a regular annual routine, there is concern that these pastoral visits could become a formality. One minister wrote: "There is also the danger—real in our churches where family visitation is a long standing practice—that family visitation degenerates into a mere formality. The necessary questions are asked; the expected answers are given. Everybody goes home heaving a sigh of relief that family visitation is over for at least another year."[69]

De Jong concedes that there are those who express:

---

67. Kleinjan, "Talks from an Elder to Elders," 20.
68. De Ruiter, "The Elder and Young Folk," 15.
69. Cammenga, "Family Visitation (2)."

> This work is necessarily fruitless because of its formal approach to spiritual life. Voices are raised in protest occasionally against the formal character of this work. They argue that since the announcement of the day and hour of the call is made . . . a conscious effort is made by every individual to present himself in the best light. All the questions are answered most cautiously. When the elders leave after an hour, they carry the impression of the family which is far from being a true reflection of what they really are.[70]

Becomes a Social Visit

In reaction to being too formal some elders have gone in the other direction. As Cammenga writes: "There is also the danger that family visitation deteriorates into a mere social visit. Where family visitation has not been totally discarded, it has often been reduced to a mere social call by the pastor and elders."[71]

Seen as Policing

Again, since home visits are "official visits," with elders often using an established set of questions there have been those who have come to regard the home visits as a form of spiritual policing. De Jong acknowledges that:

> At times the objection is raised that family visitation roots in a legalistic conception of spiritual life and the relation of the officers of the church to her members . . . On this basis the elders would act in the capacity of spiritual police with the duty of enforcing the laws. If the laws are obeyed, they may conclude that all is well. . . .the proper supervision of the members, as has been demonstrated before, must not degenerate into a system of policing and spying on the congregation.[72]

---

70. De Jong, "Objections to Family Visitation," 88.
71. Cammenga, "Family Visitation (2)."
72. De Jong, "Objections to Family Visitation," 88.

Can't Get Elders

Over the years a recurring problem has been finding men for the eldership. An Australian minister wrote in the 1960s: "It cannot be denied either that in practically all churches it is becoming more and more difficult to find men who can be considered to be fully suitable for the offices of elder."[73]

More recently an American wrote: "Our church is having difficulty finding people who will let their name stand for the position of pastoral elder because they say it is too much work."[74]

Training for Elders

There is a real dearth of training for elders in the Reformed Churches, either in the CRCA or other churches in the Reformed family around the world. A typical statement of affairs is the remark made by Langerak:

> Protestant Reformed Churches in America do little to give our elders and deacons formal, systematic training for their office. Perhaps in monthly office bearer meetings, some time is spent discussing articles of the Church Order or other relevant material. Occasionally a congregation sponsors a conference or lecture pertaining to the subject . . . but nothing formal or systematic is done to train men to be elders and deacons. Each is left to read and prepare for his work himself.[75]

A number of authors in the various Reformed or Presbyterian denominations have written workbooks to assist new elders[76] or manuals for elders to read[77] or magazines for elders.[78] The Presbyterian churches have done more to develop training for their elders, due mainly because they have life-term elders compared to the three-year terms typical of a Reformed Church. The training provided though, again tends to be readings and discussion on the church's confessions and Church Order.[79]

73. Schep, "The Biblical Requirements for Office Bearers," 10.

74. De Moor, *Job Sharing among Elders*.

75. Langerak, *Called to Serve*. See also Vander Bom, "Are Elders to be Examined?" 3–6.

76. E.g., Vanderwell, *Now That You Are an Elder*. Scipione, *Timothy, Titus and You*.

77. E.g., Hoving, "The Elder as Pastor; Home Visits." Berghoef and De Koster, *The Elders Handbook*. Tamminga, *The Elder's Handbook*.

78. E.g., *Give Yourself to Reading*, Ordained Servant.

79. Cf. for example, Hilbelink, "A Training Course for Elders and Deacon," 3–15, and 27–37. Reynolds, "A Training Program for Elders," 55–58. Wilson, "Indians,

There is very little in the way of practical training in pastoral care. As Adams has commented:

> If they are encouraged to take part in [pastoral ministry], they are given virtually no instruction in how to do so. If they are instructed at all, usually it will be in doctrine, possibly also in church government, but rarely ever in the principles and skills of personal ministry to human beings... The training that most elders lack is discipleship, or on-the-job training. They need to be taught by example.[80]

Conclusion

This literature search has delineated the history, biblical base, and purpose for the Reformed Churches' practice of pastoral care by means of home visitation by the elders. As has been demonstrated there is much value in the practice for the spiritual growth of church members when the elders fulfill their calling well.

However, the literature search has also demonstrated the many concerns about the practicalities of the home visiting system by the elders. It is also apparent that there is little done by way of a systematic and practical training for the elders in pastoral care. Thus it can be argued that a case has been established for saying there is a serious need for research into practical ways for improving the pastoral care provided by the elders and to develop some system of training for the elders.

Farmers and Church Officers," 79–80.

80. Adams, "Working With The Eldership," 27–29.

3

Methodology

Introduction

THIS CHAPTER OUTLINES THE methodology used in this research. Two methods were used, that of focus groups and that of action research.

Focus Groups

The focus groups method was used in this first part of the research because it is an ideal way to do an in-depth exploration of a topic about which little is known.[1]

Purpose

There was need to establish the validity and extent of the concerns put forward in the research question. The focus groups would also provide data as to the views of the communicant members and elders on what might constitute a reasonable way forward.

---

1. Noted by Stewart and Shamdasani, *Focus Groups; Theory and Practice*. Acknowledgement is given to Dr Jeff Pugh for suggesting the use of focus groups when reviewing the Doctor of Ministry proposal for this research as part of the Australian College of Theology Academic Committee.

Theory

The theory and practice of focus groups was researched and used to implement the focus group design.[2] Focus groups are designed to be "focused," gathering data from participants who have experienced some "particular concrete situation" which serves as the focus of the group.[3] The interaction between participants generates more information as they feel safe knowing others think the same.[4] This research focused on communicant members and elders who reflected on their own experiences with home visits.

Group Dynamics

The need to ensure the desired interaction between the focus group participants meant it was essential to consider the group dynamics in the design of the focus groups.[5] Demographic data such as age, gender, socio-economic status, ethnic background, and religion were taken into account as were the issues of group compatibility and homogeneity. The focus groups were comprised of either communicant members or elders from one local congregation. As such the participants were of similar backgrounds with a mix of genders and ages to represent the different groupings in their congregation. The participants were mostly long-term members of the local congregation, had shared many life experiences, were of the same ethnic backgrounds, and had long-term experience of the matter under consideration.

Group Size

The size of the communicant members groups was designed to be the optimum size for a focus group of eight to twelve people.[6] The elders groups consisted of the entire session for that congregation. The design accepted that the size of the elders groups might be a little under the optimal size as most sessions have a maximum of eight to nine elders, but the elders groups would thus be a single cohesive group.

---

2. For a detailed background on the theory refer to Strauss, *Qualitative Analysis for Social Scientists*. The most useful text in terms of combining theory and practice was found to be Stewart et al., *Focus Groups, Theory & Practice*. For the full set of resources consulted refer to the bibliography.

3. Stewart et al., *Focus Groups, Theory & Practice*, 9.

4. Ibid., 10–11. Cf. Brown and David, *The World Café*.

5. Stewart, *Focus Groups, Theory & Practice*, 19–35.

6. Ibid., 58.

Separating the elders and communicant members groups allowed for openness to discuss what the participants really felt in regards to the home visits provided by the elders without fear of creating unintended offence.

Environmental Influences

Consideration was given to the environmental influences which could affect the level of participation, taking into account such factors as territoriality, special arrangements, and interpersonal distance.[7] The focus groups met at their own local church building in a meeting room that comfortably held the number of participants in the respective focus groups. The participants sat around a single table in such a way that no position was seen as dominant and each participant could comfortably see one another. In each case the venue provided visual and aural privacy.

Number of Groups

The design was for eight focus groups to be conducted involving four congregations; four with communicant members and four with elders. Given that the participants were a homogeneous group it was decided that the eight groups with an estimated 70–80 participants would be sufficient to generalize to the larger church population.[8] If it was found that the responses from the participating groups were divergent then another set of groups would be organized.

Recruiting Participants

The practice in regard to focus groups is that they must consist of representative members of the larger population of interest.[9] So, to recruit participants, letters were sent to ten congregations of Classis NSW. Permission was requested to seek the participation of the communicant members and elders and an advertisement was provided for placement in the local church bulletin.

---

7. Ibid., 32–33.
8. Ibid., 44.
9. Ibid., 54.

Interview Guide

A focus group is not a brainstorming of ideas but a well planned research endeavor. The focus group interview guide sets the agenda for the focus group discussion and the questions selected constitute the construction of the research instrument.[10] The focus group interview guide finds its basis in the general research question reflecting on what is already known and what further information is required. It sets the agenda and direction for the focus group discussion. The guide is not a verbal version of a survey questionnaire but asks good questions that elicit substantial interaction amongst group members. The general formula used to design the interview guide has several principles: questions should move from the general to the specific, by order of relative importance, from the more open questions to the more directive. The number of questions should be no more than twelve and should anticipate discussion for about one and a half hours.[11]

The interview guide was designed to move from the important open question, "What is your experience of the pastoral care (home visits) provided by the elders?" to the more direct and structured question, "What do you perceive are the strengths and failings of the current system of pastoral care by the elders?" A participant's version with the five main questions was provided for the participants. A fuller researcher version was also designed with more in-depth and structured probe questions.

Focus Group Moderator

It was recognized that "an effective moderator is one of the keys to the collection of rich and valid insights from the focus groups."[12] The theory makes it clear that the focus group moderator needs to be a person who understands the nature of the research question and group dynamics. The researcher felt qualified to moderate the focus groups given he is an experienced counselor, classis chairman, and a lecturer in counseling and listening skills. The researcher also knows the research question and participants intimately.

The approach taken to moderating each focus group was, as Stewart indicates, with sensitivity and empathy balanced with detachment and

---

10. Ibid., 51. Refer to 51–67 for a full discussion of the construction of the interview guide.

11. Ibid., 61–62.

12. Ibid., 9. The theory on what makes a good focus group moderator can be found in Stewart, *Focus Groups, Theory & Practice*, 69–87. The theory is drawn from interviewing techniques, leadership studies, and group dynamics.

objectivity.[13] The interviewing was done in such a way as to ensure that participants were gently drawn into the discussion, encouraging group members to interact and build on each other's contribution. Much of the discussion flowed naturally as participants became quite involved in the issues. The main areas of the focus group guide were all covered in the time allotted.[14] The researcher was very conscious of possible bias.[15]

Recording the Discussion

Each focus group discussion was digitally recorded and reproduced verbatim for analysis. The details of that analysis can be found in the next chapter.

Action Research

The action research (AR) method was used in the second part of the research because it is a recognized way for participants to find their own way to improve their practice.

Purpose

With the focus groups providing the data of the current effectiveness of the home visitation program by the elders, the AR would then provide a mechanism for the elders to determine their own way forward.

Theory

AR as a distinct methodology began with the work of the social psychologist Kurt Lewin in the mid 1940s.[16] Two elements important to his approach were that decisions were to be made by a group and there was to be a commitment to improvement. AR, then, is a group activity involving those who are affected by the planned change and who, through the group pro-

---

13. Stewart, *Focus Groups, Theory & Practice*, 69.
14. Ibid.
15. Ibid., 85–86.
16. For a detailed history of the development of action research as a qualitative method and its epistemological foundations refer to Greenwood and Levin, *Introduction to Action Research*, 13–59, and McNiff and Whitehead *Action Research: Principles and Practice*, 3–34.

cess, take responsibility for deciding on the actions that lead to the desired improvement.[17] So, as distinct from traditional quantitative research, AR is located in the experience and context of those doing the research.[18]

The aim of AR is to improve practice rather than develop theory. It moves between action and reflection so that the one informs the other.[19] It is a process by which change and understanding can develop together. AR is cyclical with action and reflection taking place in turn. The step of reflection reviews the changes in action and thus plans the further changes to take place in the next round of action. AR is active and ongoing. It moves through the various cycles until the participants feel they have reached a satisfactory answer to their research question.[20]

AR thus moves developmentally and incrementally. The practice and understanding of the action being researched are refined over time. It can start with small cycles which help the participants define the research question more clearly.[21] Cycles may not necessarily occur in consecutive steps but may overlap, repeat, or extend previous cycles as understanding of the issues involved slowly emerges. It can take time to progress to a clearly developed and understood approach to the issue under consideration.[22]

Role of the Researcher

AR is collaborative such that a team of practitioners and a researcher work together on a project. As such it is not research *on* participants in the traditional quantitative sense of research but research *with* participants.[23] The participants in the AR team implement the research and evaluate and modify the action taken to improve their practice.[24]

The role of action researchers may be defined as being an outsider or an insider. The insiders are practitioners in the field of concern. They are usually experts well acquainted with the field of enquiry while outsiders are trained in systematic inquiry and analysis.[25] In the case of this research the

---

17. Kemmis and McTaggart, *The Action Research Planner*, 6.
18. Koshy, *Action Research for Improving Practice*, 38.
19. Crane and Richardson, *Reconnect Action Research Kit*, 1.7.
20. Ibid., 1.9.
21. Ibid.
22. Ibid. And Crane and Richardson, *Reconnect Action Research Kit*, 1.10.
23. Koshy, *Action Research for Improving Practice*, 26.
24. Cohen and Manier, "Action Research," 186.
25. Lund, *Understanding the Role of the Action Researcher*, 5.

researcher can be defined as an insider. The researcher has a history with the participants in the AR team, knows the stakeholders well, and is able to bring retrospective observations into the analysis of the issues.[26]

The researcher's role is not that of an impartial observer but a fully participating observer.[27] The researcher needed to be highly self-reflective about the research activities.[28] As an insider, having relationships with other members of the churches as well as positions of authority it was important to ensure that the responsibilities of the researcher, as well as constraints and the opinions of church members and elders, didn't bias the development by the AR team in terms of the directions they wanted to take.[29]

There was also a need to be very conscious that the participants in the AR team were allowed to define and set their own directions in a collaborative effort without the researcher directing the research and the participants simply becoming consumers of knowledge given by the researcher rather than being the knowledge producers.[30]

The role of the researcher was to assist the participants to move forward to find a mutually agreeable outcome. To achieve that outcome it required the adoption of a variety of roles at various stages including: planner, leader, facilitator, catalyzer, listener, observer, synthesizer, and reporter.[31] As the researcher in this AR process, assistance was given to help the AR team process change. Assistance was given to reflect back to the participants on the way things were being done and the implications of their planning. Using skills of reflective listening and Socratic questioning participants were assisted to understand their own responses and make their own self-reflections. The researcher helped make evident the tacit knowledge that guided the participants' actions. So, in summary the researcher functioned as a coach regarding the participants as talented players and helping them come to their own conclusions in terms of better practice for their ministry.[32]

---

26. Holian, "Doing Research in my Own Organization," 8.
27. Ibid., 3.
28. Lund, *Understanding the Role of the Action Researcher*, 9.
29. Holian, "Doing Research in my Own Organization," 8.
30. Lund, *Understanding the Role of the Action Researcher*, 5.
31. O'Brien, *An Overview of the Methodological Approach*, 10.
32. Greenwood and Levin, *Introduction to Action Research*, 124–127.

Validation

It was the intention of the researcher to establish findings that could be used across the board by elders of the CRCA; that is, the findings could be generalized. It has often been argued that AR only provides anecdotal evidence in a particular context or that it improves practice in the particular setting in which it is conducted and does not provide knowledge for a broader setting.[33] That being the case, the researcher identified a need to establish the validity of the research findings.

In AR the basis for validation is the conscious and deliberate enactment of the AR cycle,[34] thus the notion of "recoverability." This offers a way for others to follow the route of the AR or "recovering" the research process so the outcomes are understandable.[35] To aid in this the researcher made use of monitoring techniques to allow the reader to recover the research process and the outcomes. To that end, digital recordings were made of all AR team meetings and reproduced verbatim.

Validation in AR also includes the testing of key arguments with a critical audience to identify where there is a lack of clarity and ensuring that any claims to new knowledge are fair in relation to the data. To that end the researcher produced a position paper for the AR team when it was close to a satisfactory outcome. This document was then distributed to numerous sessions, individual elders, and ministers for critique. Interviews were conducted with sessions on the basis of the document and the critique incorporated into the AR process.

One further step used to assist in ensuring or determining the validity of the research was to follow the systemic approach provided by the mnemonic PEArL.[36] As well as being a tool that can be used by the reader to appraise the research and evaluate the validity of the findings, the researcher used the five aspects of this approach in the design of this research.

---

33. Champion and Stowell, "Validating Action Research Field Studies: PEArL," 25.

34. Coghlan, "Action Research in the Academy," 3.

35. Champion and Stowell, "Validating Action Research Field Studies: PEArL," 21.

36. Ibid., 21–36.

Participants

By definition, AR involves as participants those who are themselves involved in the problem situation of the field of enquiry.[37] The criteria for inclusion as participants in the AR involved the following: the participants were to be elders of good standing in their respective congregations, either currently serving in their three-year term in office or out of office between the three-year terms.[38] There was to be a representation of those who had long experience of the home visitation program, who knew well the requirements of the home visiting system, those who knew the elders' and communicant members' expectations, and were aware of the value and limitations of the home visiting approach to pastoral care. The participants were also to represent the younger generation of elders as well as the ethnic mix and socio-economic mix of the congregations.

Engagement

It was recognized that engaging people within a collaborative enquiry process and ongoing commitment to the purpose of this research would not be easy.[39] The qualifications or expertise required for the participants to be involved in the research was that they had experience in conducting pastoral home visits in the CRCA and had a good knowledge of the biblical and confessional background of pastoral care in the CRCA as well as the requirements of the Church Order.

The participants were to be those who felt secure in terms of appreciating the pastoral care approach by the CRCA elders yet were open to possible change of that system if the data and their considerations warranted such a change. The participants were under no constraints to maintain the current system or to reach some predetermined outcome.

The participants were able to meet together regularly at a convenient time and place of their own choosing. The participants received all the resources and documentation they required from the researcher or they had, or obtained, their own resources which were also used as input. No participant was appointed to participate by any session or encouraged by any lobby group within the churches. Each volunteered of their own accord after receiving information and orientation as to the nature of the research.

---

37. Ibid., 28.
38. Refer to the glossary for the definition of elders detailing this distinction.
39. Champion and Stowell, "Validating Action Research Field Studies: PEArL," 29.

Authority

It is important to determine under what authority the research was undertaken. Reflection on who authorized the research and for what reasons assists the reader in judging the authenticity and objectivity of the research.[40]

This research was initiated by the researcher under the auspices of the Australian College of Theology. No session or classis requested the research to be undertaken nor did any particular church lobby group or concerned communicant members. The origin of the research derived from the researcher's years of instructing and mentoring elders and sensing their frustrations at not being able to provide care in a manner most conducive to the spiritual well-being of the communicant members under their oversight.

relationships[41]

It is necessary to consider the relationships involved in and affected by the AR.[42] AR being a collaborative process, account needed to be taken of the assumptions and beliefs of the participants as well as those affected by the outcomes of the research which could cause misunderstanding, even strong disagreement.

The participants recognized that while they had a variety of experience of pastoral care as elders, and varied professional and skills backgrounds, as well as their ethnic backgrounds, there was a common commitment to the teachings of the CRCA confessions. Especially pertinent was their common commitment to adhere to the biblical requirements concerning the issues involved in this research.

The participants reviewed the data of the focus groups and the AR process and were determined that, given the constraints of the Bible, the practical out-workings of the research would be allowed to stand on their own merits. The participants did not come with any preconceived notions of a need to change, nor of a need to maintain the status quo if the data suggested a need for change and the Bible did not disallow such a change.

---

40. Ibid., 29–30.

41. Please note, the word "relationships" has been deliberately left in the lower case. As Champion and Stowell put it "we perceive the 'relationships' element of the PEArL mnemonic as being of *prime* importance when reflecting on the character of the inquiry. We have designated the 'r' as being lowercase, to bring attention to this element and to reflect a 'soft' interpretivist approach to the issue of power within a situation." Ibid., 30. Italics in the original.

42. Champion and Stowell, "Validating Action Research Field Studies: PEArL," 31.

It was recognized that if the participants determined by means of the AR process that a change in the elders' pastoral care method was appropriate that such a determination could cause concern, perhaps even a conflict of conscience within certain elements of the churches. However, the following considerations allowed the participants to approach the research without feeling obligated to hold to any position. The research was independent of any official direction from the local churches or classis. The findings of the AR team would not be binding on the churches. On the other hand if the research findings were to have any benefit in the churches they would need to be adopted by the respective churches. One approach for such adoption would be by means of the scrutiny of the AR results and debate at the various assemblies of the CRCA. The other approach considered would be for the results of the AR to be seen as an alternative that local churches were free to adopt, especially if such aligned with their local circumstances. Thus respecting the autonomy of the elders in the local congregations, any development of the AR findings would be gradual and organic.

It was also noted that if the communicant members and elders of any local congregation recognized the intent and findings of the research through the "recoverability" of this research and the use of public critique as part of the AR process, there would be a greater appreciation of the research.

Learning

The collaborative nature of the AR process meant there would be a group of participants who would meet regularly over an extended period of time. So a high degree of method and orderliness was needed to obtain and hold onto what was learned.[43]

In the design of this research it was estimated that the AR process would take six months. Given that length of time, it was necessary for the researcher to ensure a strict adherence to the AR process and a clear methodology in terms of reflecting upon and holding on to the emerging findings. To that end the researcher recorded each meeting of the AR team and then provided the participants with a full verbatim record of each meeting. The researcher also provided copies of the diary notes, observation notes by the participants, as well as summaries and implication questions for the participants. This detail allowed the participants to reflect on the cyclical nature of the AR process as well as come to conclusions based on the accumulation of ideas, observations, and reflections that built upon each other over time.

---

43. Ibid., 31–32.

AR Cycles

The four-stage AR cycle, was adhered to in the design of the research. This ongoing cycle is detailed as follows:

PLAN

AR planning involved deciding on how to respond to the research question and what action to try out. The plan would need to be specific.

The first step would involve a consideration of the research question in the context of the focus group data and the theory or theology of elders' pastoral care by means of home visitation. In the context of this research any plan devised would need to be limited to the framework set by the CRCA confessions and biblical understandings.

The second step would involve what would actually be put into action. There could be numerous possibilities to trial but not everything could be trialed and certainly not at once. So, strategic decisions would need to be made as to what were the most significant issues and what single action could have the most powerful effect. As the AR process is an ongoing cycle, no attempt would be made to find a solution in one trial. But on the other hand, what is tried should not be insignificant but should have substantial practical and theoretical significance.

The third step at this point would be to plan for the observation stage, which often runs concurrently with the action phase, to monitor what has occurred. The AR team would need to decide how to record the action and what resources would be needed to monitor the action being trialed.[44]

ACT

In the action phase the participants implement the plan as designated in the previous phase. In the case of this research the implementation would be conducted by the AR team in the actual setting of providing pastoral care in their local congregations.

In implementing the planned changes it is always hoped that the desired improvements would occur. But whether they did or not, the results of the planned action needed to be monitored as they occurred and thus became grist for the mill in the next cycle. Whatever results occurred would give insights for improvement in the next cycle. It was noted in this design

---

44. Crane and Richardson, *Reconnect Action Research Kit*, 2.5–2.9.

that the action planned did not need to be complex. It might involve a small change at first for testing ideas and developing an initial strategy.[45]

Observe

In designing this research it was recognized that good observation requires looking at what is happening during the action phase and describing it accurately. The purpose of the observing phase was to provide a sound base for reflection. It was recognized that the best ideas that develop the research could come when least expected. The observations would need to collect both the positive and negative aspects in relation to the planned improvement. Planned action, which was identified as not improving practice, would provide useful insight for the next rounds of the AR cycle. In the design of this research the following techniques for monitoring were regarded as most useful: anecdotal records including written descriptive records of what an individual did or said in the action phase; diaries, which include the participants' observations, feelings, reactions, interpretations, reflections, hunches, and hypotheses; interviews; group brainstorming; and digital recording.[46]

Reflect

This phase is about the participants acquiring a shared understanding of the meaning of what happened. Reflection informs the improvements to be designed at the next planning phase and it would either affirm or challenge particular ways of doing things. In a sense the reflection involves developing a "theory" about what happened. This would be achieved by the participants brainstorming the issues, sharing insights, and piecing things together.

It was recognized that change had the possibility of developing a certain amount of incompetence. There would be the possibility that the participants would not have mastered the skills needed for the new way of providing pastoral care that they would begin to envisage was needed. Through the reflection participants would not only have a clearer idea of what to do next, but also what they needed to learn if they were to do better in the next round of the AR cycle. The next phase might thus include not only what changed action was required, but planning how they would learn the new or enhanced skills required. It was noted that learning what

---

45. Ibid., 2.9.
46. Ibid., 2.10–2.11.

needs to be learned is one of the most important outcomes of the reflection stage.[47]

This reflection by the participants would then also need to consider such things as change management in how the churches rethink their pastoral care methodology. If the AR team would need to learn new skills as it went through the AR cycles, then even more so for the churches which have not been through that process. It was recognized that a certain approach to pastoral care is shaped by history, traditions, long-standing expectations, and so on. The AR process may well have been structured on a different set of premises than the previous system of pastoral care because the current circumstances are different.

---

47. Ibid., 2.11–2.13.

4

Analysis of the Focus Groups

Introduction

IN THIS CHAPTER A summation and interpretation will be provided of the results of the focus groups.

Eight focus groups were conducted over a two-month period. They provide a sample of the views of the communicant members and elders of the Christian Reformed Church of Australia (CRCA) in regards to the pastoral care provided by the elders by means of home visiting. Four focus groups were conducted with communicant members and four with the elders.

The findings were very consistent across the focus groups. It was therefore deemed that these eight focus groups would provide a sufficient sample for the research. Anecdotal evidence from various sources also was consistent with the focus group data.[1]

The focus group discussions were all digitally recorded and transcribed verbatim.

---

1. Anecdotal evidence has already been established in chapter 1. Further anecdotal evidence was found in an international comparison to focus groups. Refer to the appendix for obtaining details.

Focus Group Participants

A total of thirty-nine participants was involved with the communicant members focus groups; the average age being 48.9 years with a range of 18–83 years of age. The average number of years that these participants were members of their church was 32.3 years with a range of 1–57 years. The male to female ratio was 14/25 participants. For the elders focus groups a total of twenty-eight participants was involved; the average age being 53.9 years with a range of 35–77 years of age. The average number of years that these participants were members of their church was 35.8 years with a range of 3–64 years.[2]

This data indicates that the focus groups have a good cross section of the ages of communicant members with a tendency towards long-term membership in the churches. There is a predominance of females in the communicant membership sample, which assists to balance the male-only elders sample. The higher average age of the elders reflects that the eldership in the CRCA tends towards the older men of the congregations. The high average length of time in the congregation demonstrates that the views expressed in the focus group data are that of long-term mature members and elders.

Analysis of the Data

The data obtained from the eight focus groups was assessed using a standard qualitative or ethnographic summary methodology. Verbatim records were produced of the eight focus groups. From these records two sets of collated responses were produced, one for the communicant members focus groups and one for the elders focus groups. These provide the data for the focus group summary analysis.[3] The rest of this chapter will delineate the findings of that summary analysis.

Purpose of Home Visits

The initial question on the focus group participant guide asked the participants to give their view as to the purpose of the home visits provided by the elders of their church.

---

2. Refer to the appendix for obtaining details.
3. Refer to the appendix for details.

The communicant members focus groups generated sixteen responses across the four churches and the gender and age groups. Apart from one negative response all responses were positive in expressing the purpose for home visits.

There was an even spread over the notions of encouragement, relationships, and oversight. There was acknowledgement that it was part of the responsibility of the elders to have oversight of the church members, to assess their personal walk with God, provide prayer and support for them, and help them reach their potential in the church. This oversight involved good relationships, someone to listen to them, and someone who knew them and expressed interest. Encouragement was seen as an important facet of the oversight.

The elders focus groups expressed similar views with eighteen responses recorded on this issue, spread across the four churches and the age groups. The elders exhibited a greater use of the notion of oversight, but also that of encouragement and relationships. The elders expressed the purpose of home visits as assisting in the supervision of the church community: the session being able to keep a loving eye over the congregation. Good relationships were seen as essential, the elders seeing themselves as being responsible to know their members more intimately and to share in their experiences of life. It was stated that elders should be encouraging their members, challenging them, and helping nurture them in their Christian walk.

Experience of Home Visits

The follow-up question in the opening section of the focus group guide was an open question asking participants to share their experience of the home visits they had received or had provided as elders. What is significant in reviewing the responses to this question is how quickly and extensively the responses indicate a range of concerns in regards to the actual experience of the home visits provided by elders in contrast to the purpose the groups had just stated. The number and range of responses were such that several distinct issues could be categorized as discussed below.

Relationships

Seven communicant members across the four churches and the gender and age groups remarked that they didn't know their elders when they provided a home visit. Because of that lack of relationship they expressed they felt uncomfortable and were hesitant to really share with the elders.

The elders focus group had thirty-two responses across the four churches raising the matter of relationships. The majority acknowledged that the general relationship with the church members was not there. It was acknowledged that there was pressure from the Church Order, which specified annual visits regardless of the existing relationships. There was also a significant number expressing concern that there was a tendency towards lack of trust and respect for the elders. Members were not always taking it as a given that an elder was appointed by God and thus should be one with whom church members could and should share their faith and concerns.

Frequency of Visits

Eleven communicant members across the four churches made remarks on this category. The majority expressed the concern that one visit per year, even if provided, was not enough; a person could not really confide in someone that was seen once per year. Those commenting on the regularity of the annual visits were divided between those who had received visits annually and those who received visits every three to four years

There were ten responses from the elders focus groups across the four churches on this issue of the frequency of home visits. All four churches admitted the elders found it increasingly difficult to achieve annual visits with all their church members. Elders who were fully employed struggled to provide annual visits as distinct to those elders retired from employment. The responses also made clear there was a tendency to consider using small groups for pastoral care instead of the annual home visits.

Training

Eleven responses from the communicant members from two churches and across the age and gender groups expressed concern about the lack of training for elders. They acknowledged the elders meant well but were not doing what was required due to lack of training such as handling pastoral issues properly.

The elders focus groups also generated eleven responses under this category across three churches and the age groups. It was expressed that finding suitable men was very difficult, that too often those nominated for the office of elder were not suitable. Several elders admitted to not being qualified to handle pastoral difficulties, that they had never been trained or had never received a home visit themselves to know what it involved.

Routine

Eight responses from communicant members across three churches expressed a view to the effect that home visits had become routine, a "tick-the-box" exercise. The elders focus groups also generated eight responses across three churches expressing concern the home visitation program had become routine, one cause being attributed to the Church Order that required annual visits. Elders noted communicant members can tend to see the visits as a formal process and just go through the motions.

Follow-up

Three responses from the communicant members focus groups across two churches expressed concern that after the yearly visit there was no follow-up on the issues raised.

Two elders from their focus groups mentioned this item; one admitting being delinquent in follow-up after a visit and the other was concerned that reporting to the session on home visits may deter a church member's willingness to be open in their discussions at the home visit.

Generation/Gender

There were nine responses from the communicant members focus groups across three churches and across the age and gender groups that expressed the concern that it was difficult for the younger members and female members to relate with elders who tended to be older males.

The elders focus groups generated thirty responses relating to generational differences across the four churches. No gender issues were raised. Amongst the responses, the issues raised were that the older generation appreciated home visits, but the younger generation didn't understand the system and perceived it as policing. The younger generation perceived elders differently such that the elders' standing lacked authority. The elders found it difficult to keep up with the changes and provide answers to the questions of the younger generation.

Method/Perception

This issue related generally to how the elders did their ministry or how the method was perceived. Twenty responses from the communicant members focus groups were identified across the four churches. From these responses several subcategories were discerned. One was that members expressed that they felt scrutinized, that home visits were a policing of the members visited. It was felt that the home visits should be more informal. A further group of responses expressed that home groups would be a better approach to pastoral care.

The elders focus groups generated thirty-three responses on this issue across the four churches. A large segment of responses was concerned that the elders were perceived as policemen checking up on members. Another large group of responses dealt with the question of how the Holy Spirit was involved in a home visit and how the elder should work with that. The remaining third of the responses under this heading were evenly divided across the issues of whether home groups were better for pastoral care, concerns that church members did not really share matters with the elders, and concerns with the system itself. This last item raised the concern about the lack of continuity given that elders retire from office after three years. On a positive note it was also expressed that at least there is pastoral care provided by elders, the point being made that other denominations have little or no pastoral care for their members.

These numerous concerns were listed in response to an open question about the experiences of those who had received home visits or provided home visits as elders. While there were those who appreciated being visited by the elders or enjoyed doing the home visits as elders, the clear majority of the matters raised expressed reservations about the system before the weaknesses of the system were probed, which comes up in the next section.

Perceived Strengths and Weaknesses of the Current System

This was an open-ended question regarding the participants' perceptions on the strengths and weaknesses of the current system of pastoral care, namely home visiting by the elders.

Strengths

Seven responses were received from the communicant members focus groups across three churches, predominantly from older members. The main strength was that the church members did get visited and the system linked every person with a pastoral carer. The visits were especially encouraging when conducted at a time of need, for example, when a member was in hospital.

Six responses from the elders focus groups were identified over two churches which mentioned that the system provided a structure for pastoral care and accountability. It was useful to have retired elders to visit the elderly in the congregation.

Weaknesses

The communicant members focus groups generated four responses from one church that can be listed under this general heading. The issues mentioned included the age difference between an old elder and a young person being visited, not always feeling at ease with certain elders, and doubts about trusting the elders given they will report on the home visit to the session. The need for elders and communicant members to be educated as to what home visits were about was also expressed.

Nineteen responses from the elders focus groups were identified from two churches. One church focused on the lack of a personal relationship between elders and church members. This, coupled with a perceived mindset that elders had a policing role, made home visits less than fruitful. The fact that home visits were made once a year without a trusting relationship and with pointed questions, exacerbated the perception of policing by the elders. The other church focused its discussion on the concern that the current home visiting system assumed things that no longer exist. For example the village community where the elders knew their people well and saw them regularly.

The focus groups participant guide targeted questions on seven specific issues.

Lack of Time

The communicant members groups generated eighteen responses across three churches and across the age and gender groups to the question, "How much of the elders' lack of pastoral care is due to lack of time, longer working hours?" These responses indicate a number of issues including: length of time elders are tied up with their employment and travel time (traffic problems), and having only evenings to do home visits due to full-time employment and involvement in other church programs. Further responses included church members cancelling home visits and thus wasting elders' time, the need to have two elders on a home visit, and thus doubling up on the number of people they need to visit.

The elders focus groups produced eighteen responses across the four churches on this issue. The concerns listed included: time involved in their employment and all the other church programs; the need for time with their own families; and the need for the families to accept the time requirements for elders and support them in the need to be away from the family. Church members also have less time to receive elders for home visits. On the other hand there was also an emphasis for elders to be aware of their calling to make time to fulfill their role.

Lack of Training

Fifteen responses from the communicant members focus groups across the four churches and the age and gender groups were received in response to the question, "How much of the elders' lack of pastoral care is due to lack of training?" A good portion of the responses referred directly to the fact they felt elders lacked training or they shared experiences of new elders being unprepared and intimidated by their task. On the other side were a couple of responses that assumed if the elders had grown up in the Reformed Churches they should know how to provide home visits. Others advised that new elders should team up with the older, experienced elders, or they should be trained by the minister. A final response was that the communicant members should also be educated as to the value and process of home visits.

The elders focus groups generated twenty-five responses categorized under this issue across the four churches. Just over a third of those responses admitted the elders lacked training acknowledging it was a major issue. It was expressed that typically men were voted into office unprepared and then spent the first two years of a three-year term coming to grips with what they were supposed to do. That left one year to be fairly useful in the role before the elder's term was over. Just over another third of the responses dealt with suggestions for training, the majority suggesting new elders be teamed up with a senior elder and mentored by him. Another concern was the fact that there were new elders who just did not have the talent/gifts for the office.

Lack of Community

Twelve responses from across the four churches were received from the communicant members focus groups in response to the question, "How much of the elders' lack of pastoral care is due to lack of community; they don't really know you?" Some responses simply stated "people don't know each other." Others expressed there was a lack of community due to the distance members lived from each other, living in different suburbs 20–30 minutes away from each other. So there was no sense of a communal village. References were made to how church members used to compensate for this lack of community by inviting each other for coffee after church, a practice that was diminishing. Others suggested they were compensating for the lack of community through small groups. One response admitted there was a need to think of different ways to get back the fellowship that was missing.

The elders focus groups had ten responses across three churches on this issue. All three churches identified that there was a lack of community. Each also said that they compensated for that lack of community by having small groups. One church added that they had further compensation by the members meeting each other at church programs or catching up at the Christian school.

Reactive Versus Proactive Care

Only three responses from one church were received from the communicant members focus groups in response to the question, "How much of the elders' lack of pastoral care is due to focusing on reactive care; problems instead of proactive discipling?" The discussion admitted that the members would appreciate more proactive discipling, but suggested the busyness of their schedules implied only the reactive care could be given.

The elders focus groups similarly only received four responses from the one church. Their discussion revolved around whether home visits could be seen as reactive or proactive care. If the visits encouraged church members and strengthened their faith then they were seen as proactive.

An Outdated Approach

The communicant members focus groups generated eighteen responses across three churches to the question, "How much of the elders' lack of pastoral care is due to using an outdated approach that is seen as intrusive and irrelevant?" A fifth, younger communicant members, stated they felt home visits were intrusive. Others expressed the concern that the younger members had not had good experiences with home visits and thus saw them as intrusive. Those who expressed that the home visits were irrelevant included such things as there was no follow-up, that it was better to be visited by the minister, and that small groups were the better way to go. One of the responses argued that the CRCA was in decline, which provided the evidence that its methods were outdated and irrelevant.

The elders focus group responses to this question were subsumed under the next question.

Response to Elders' Handbook Quote

The focus groups were asked to respond to the following quote and question, "An elders' handbook says of the elder that 'their office demands that each diligently keep watch over his own parish . . . this shall be done especially close to the time of celebration of the Lord's Supper. The [elders] shall faithfully investigate whether the church members manifest themselves uprightly in walk and conduct, in their duties of godliness . . . the [elders] shall admonish them.' How do you relate to that approach by the elders?"

The communicant members focus groups generated thirteen responses across two churches. One church was positive in regards to the quote, stating the concepts were good though the language was not current. It argued that the church would be in a better condition if the concepts in the quote were still adhered to. It was important that elders kept watch over themselves and provided a good role model for the congregation. The other church was more negative towards the quote expressing that the language and concepts were archaic. The importance of the elders' oversight was recognized, but home visits provided once a year or once in two years was pointless because the elders didn't really know much about the doctrine and life of the church members.

The elders focus groups generated twenty-four responses across the four churches. More than half disagreed with the quote. There were those who felt it was irrelevant given the geographical spread of the congregation with elders not knowing what was really happening in the lives of their members. Others admitted they had let things slip, that the approach was seen as policing, or that the approach in the past had generated fear. Those who expressed a more positive view said the concepts in the quote were good but needed to be done in a positive way, that there needed to be a change of style. It was admitted that the concepts were correct but that elders avoided them. It was also expressed that the congregations needed to know about church discipline.

Age and Gender Differences

In response to the question, "Given that CRCA elders are all (older?) males, how does that affect how you receive pastoral care if you are a female or a younger communicant member?" Eleven responses were identified from the communicant members focus groups from two churches. Four responses, mainly older females, saw no problems with having an older male. But three responses by younger members did express a concern with having an older elder visit them. The age difference was seen to affect the elders' understanding of the younger members' issues. Little or no concern was expressed on the gender issue, one church remarking that they have female pastoral carers.

Six responses across three churches were received from the elders focus groups on this question. There was little concern over the gender difference. Elders suggested that the difference could be compensated for with proper planning and the use of female pastoral carers. There was concern expressed by the younger elders that there was a relationship gap between the older and younger generations and that the way things were tackled 20–30 years ago would not be effective for the new generation which expected something different.

Conclusions

The data above raises serious concerns about the effectiveness of the system in the current context. This is emphasized by the fact that many of the issues probed in this section were already alluded to by church members and elders in the previous section with the initial open question. What further emphasizes these concerns is that there is a consistency of views, not only across the churches and age and gender groups, but also across both the communicant members and elders focus groups. The elders admit to the same issues in the same way and to the same extent as that expressed in the communicant members focus groups.

New Testament Teaching on Pastoral Care

In this section of the focus group guide the focus of the discussion revolved around the questions, "If we think about what the New Testament says about the shepherding role of the elders, what does it say about *how* the elders are to fulfill their role? Is the current mode of pastoral care listed in the Church Order the only way it can be done if we follow the New Testament?"

Twenty-eight responses across the four churches were identified from the communicant members focus groups dealing with this question. Just over a third of these responses stated that the New Testament does not say how the elders are to fulfill their role. Another third, agreeing with the previous remark, said the New Testament focuses on the character of those providing pastoral care. A small number admitted they didn't know what the New Testament teaches and another small number, while agreeing the New Testament does not state elders must do home visits, expressed the need for caution in how changes might be made. It was acknowledged that the Church Order, which refers to annual home visits by elders, is how the denomination has agreed to do it. However, there is room to do things differently provided there is adherence to what the Bible teaches. Such things as fellowship, prayer, and studying the Bible together were seen as things to consider in regards to what the Bible teaches on another approach.

The elders focus groups generated fifty-four responses on this question across the four churches. Just over a third said clearly the New Testament does not say how elders are to fulfill their role. A quarter of the responses agreed and said what the New Testament teaches relates to character issues. Those character issues were identified as watching over one's own spiritual growth, having humility and being aware of one's own failings, being a role model, and having integrity. Further responses dealing with a methodology listed things such as: elders having oversight, being spiritual shepherds, protecting the flock, prayer, and being role models. Again there were a number of responses expressing the need to be careful of changing the system of care provided by the elders. It was suggested that wise men had developed a tradition of care over hundreds of years that should not all be thrown out. The question was how to achieve what the church fathers achieved but now in the current time and context.

The "One Another" Passages

Twenty-nine responses were received across the four churches from the communicant members focus groups to the question, "What about all the 'one another' passages in the New Testament—is pastoral care more what we do for one another? How would the elders fit in with that?" Three quarters of those responses affirmed that pastoral care is what church members do for each other. Two thirds of that group of responses focused on care provided by way of cell groups. The other third of those responses referred to a combination of care provided for each other with that provided by the elders. The key notion was that pastoral care is the duty of each church member. The awareness of each others' needs and the capacity to care worked best by way of the cell groups.

The elders focus groups generated twelve responses to this question across three churches. All agreed that pastoral care is what should be done by and for each other. Just under half of the responses expressed the requirement that elders should be trained and lead by example. Another third suggested care for each other should be combined with home visits by elders. It was stated that the Christian principle was that church members should care for each other and that the elders should model it to the congregation.

Summary

From the data above it can be seen that there is agreement, across the churches and also by the communicant members and elders focus groups, that the New Testament does not specify how pastoral care must be done, so it allows for change to current practices as long as the elders focus on being spiritual shepherds of God's people.

Current System in Twenty-First-Century Australia

In this section of the focus group guide the participants were asked to discuss the question, "How would you respond to the suggestion that the current system of pastoral care by the elders does not relate to the current generation in twenty-first-century Australia?"

Responses to this question were only received from two elders focus groups, mainly due to the fact that that the other focus groups felt the issues had been covered under previous questions.

Thirty-eight responses were tabulated from the two elders focus groups. These responses focused on the issues of the failure of the Church Order in the current setting, generational differences, and cultural differences. The cultural issue was identified as being the difference between the Dutch and Australian cultures. The need for relationships was also referred to. A summary view expressed that there was a difference between two models, one focusing on authority and the other on being a servant based on relationships. Responses suggesting what was needed referred to the elder's character and cell groups. It was stated that there can be change but the gospel must not be changed.

Brainstorming Another Method

In this final section of the focus group guide the participants were asked to explore what a new approach to pastoral care by the elders might look like. The initial question in this section was, "Considering the biblical principles, and given a chance to brainstorm/dream, what would be the ideal method of pastoral care that would assist the church members under your pastoral care to grow spiritually mature, help them to witness/disciple/minister for the Lord?"

Twenty-eight responses from the communicant members focus groups were identified on this question from two churches. Over a third of these responses referred to mentoring or other relational issues such as sharing experiences, encouraging, hospitality, and having prayer partners. It was expressed that there is a need to start seeing role models: a lifestyle by elders that models for the members what the desired Christian life is like. A significant group suggested spiritual growth came about through doing mission: being involved in some form of ministry. Another group of responses stated there was a need for better management by elders who have too many things to get on top of. And there was a need for guidelines for elders to make space for pastoral care. One response called for flexibility in pastoral care depending on the preferences of the members. However, it was important to identify how those various approaches were connected to the elders who have oversight of the congregation.

The elders focus groups generated twenty-seven responses to this question across three churches. Again, one of the largest groups of responses related to mentoring, including accountability for prayer and Bible reading. The biblical model of Paul and Timothy was cited as an example of the more mature Christian taking the less mature Christian under their wing and working and training with them. The other group of responses by the elders referred to developing pastoral teams where a team of men and women could be involved in conducting visits to complement the elders' visiting program. Reference was also made to involving the deacons or a full-time pastoral carer. Having church members involved in a mission or church ministry was also raised. The need to separate the leadership and pastoral care roles of the elders was also mentioned. These were seen as separate spiritual gifts and few were good at both.

Teaching from Ephesians 4

The question here was, "What does the Bible mean in Ephesians 4 when it speaks of 'pastors and teachers (elders) preparing God's people for works of service so that the body of Christ may be built up until we all reach unity in the faith and in the knowledge of the Son of God and become mature, attaining to the whole measure of the fullness of Christ.' (Ephesians 4:11–13)?" Very few responses were received here with only one church discussing the question directly. For the others the answer to the question was obvious, needing no articulation and/or the discussion was subsumed under that of the next question.

Two responses from one church were received from the communicant members focus groups. The emphasis of the responses was on the task of the elders being to prepare the people for ministry such that they mature and attain to the measure of Christ.

Four responses were received from the elders focus groups from the same church. The responses were the same as with the communicant members group with the addition that the elders group admitted that elders can be so busy running themselves ragged trying to do everything when such is not their calling.

Defining Spiritual Maturity

Fourteen responses were received from the communicant members groups across the four churches to the question, "What in your opinion is spiritual maturity? What do you think are the indicators of growth towards maturity?" A significant group of responses defined spiritual maturity as becoming more like Christ, focusing on him, witnessing for him. Another aspect of developing maturity was bearing fruit, growing in understanding and self-feeding; mature Christians are those who feed themselves on God's Word and become more aware of the richness God has given. Trusting God and remaining joyful in the midst of suffering was the third main area of defining Christian maturity. The fourth area was that those growing spiritually serve others.

The elders focus groups generated twenty-five responses across the four churches. Very similar areas to the communicant members groups were listed by the elders, the difference being in the order of highest number of responses to a category. Over a third of the elders' responses listed serving others and use of gifts as indicators of spiritual maturity. The next highest group said having God as the main objective of a person's life; depending on him was an expression of spiritual maturity. This was followed by those who said spiritual maturity meant becoming more like Christ. Being fruitful and regular with devotions was also listed.

Actions by Elders to Assist Spiritual Growth

Thirty-four responses were received from the communicant members focus groups from across the four churches to the question, "What actions and attitudes do elders need to have to assist church members in achieving spiritual growth?" By far the category with the highest number of responses referred directly to mentoring. When the associated concepts are included with mentoring nearly two thirds of the responses relate to the general idea of mentoring. The associated concepts include modeling life, realizing an elder is always an elder, providing accountability, honest sharing, and encouragement and praying for people. There was a clear expression of the need for elders to challenge and encourage the members, to walk alongside them and ask good questions, to provide resources.

The next group of ideas related to the concept of training, using various learning styles, providing men's fellowships. The final group of ideas related generally to the system of how elders do their task: things like not policing, not setting up obstacles, delegating session business, limiting the number of people elders are asked to relate to, and having effective handovers when elders finish their term of office. There was concern that much of what the elders do as a session they should not actually be doing.

Thirty-one responses were identified in the elders focus groups relating to this question. Over a third of those related to an extended discussion in one church on the value of having church members involved in mission projects. The final conclusion was that the elders need to have the church members be obedient to God and to his call. The side-benefit of involving members in ministry was that the church members would grow spiritually by taking on the challenge God put before them.

Apart from the extended discussion on involvement in missions, the key item for elders to assist in the spiritual growth of the church members again revolved around the ideas of mentoring and modeling the faith. An astute observation in the responses stated that the need for mentoring was high due to what had been lost in the current cultural setting. In the past church families lived in village type settings with extended families providing modeling and mentoring of the faith. The annual home visiting by elders was useful because of the frequent opportunities to relate at other times. The current system was failing because the various aspects of a previous cultural environment that underpinned the system were no longer there. It was stated that small groups were necessary to develop relationships and community, and also for the opportunity to observe elders modeling the faith. And mentoring was needed to assist in the personal development and growth of individuals.

Developing the CRCA Vision

The final question stated:

> Our denominational Synod in 2006 adopted a Vision Statement entitled *A Church Reforming to Reach the Lost for Christ*. It was decided that our congregations needed to work on four areas: *1. spiritual fervor and prayer life, a life that is exemplified in its desire to live a holy life and has a passion for the lost; 2. outreach and church planting, where churches are encouraged to do far more in terms of personal evangelism and planting new churches; 3. training, where the churches consider how they can develop training for church members in their ministry; 4. changing structures, where the churches rethink how they do things so they are better able to do the above three.* Considering point 4 how might the proactive pastoral care provided by elders help us in achieving the first three?

Thirty-nine responses were identified from the communicant members focus groups across the four churches in relation to this question. A quarter of the responses said they didn't know the vision or their church didn't have what the vision called for. Half the respondents stated direct action was needed by the elders, most saying the elders needed training to be able to assist the churches make any advancement on the goals of the vision, the rest saying the elders should lead by example or they need to be praying. The final segment of responses listed individual ideas on how the elders could assist with the achievement of the goals of the vision: encouraging involvement, setting goals, adopting the models of other churches, considering new structures, as well as elders networking by means of small groups, and involvement with the community.

The elders focus groups generated twenty-four responses across the four churches in their discussion of this question. More than a third of these responses related to their view on the vision, most of the responses recognizing the need for change, though it might be difficult, with a segment also arguing that no change was needed. A third recognized the need for training for the elders to affect the changes needed to develop the vision. Most of the responses suggested that elders needed to disciple each other and that the congregation also needed training. A small segment of the responses said the younger members of the congregations were better at what the vision was focused on and they were also more outward looking. A final small segment said there was need for consistent preaching and prayer and the power of the Spirit for there to be advancement in terms of the goals of the vision.

Summary

What is seen from the data is the consistency of the views of the participants across the four churches and also between the communicant members and elders focus groups

In consideration of the ideal method for pastoral care the various segments of the section came to a repeated refrain: the need for mentoring by the elders, to have their lives seen as models of the Christian faith, was the main concept put forward. Also strong was the desire for elders to provide discipleship training and involvement in mission projects and ministry. Development of pastoral care teams was also considered useful.

International Comparison

An opportunity was provided for the researcher to discuss his research with ministers and seminary lecturers with a North American denomination, which is in ecclesiastical fellowship with the CRCA and has a similar confessional, ethnic, and church polity background. The notes from the interviews provide an opportunity to compare the findings of this research with that of a comparative setting.[4]

The ministers and theological lecturers made it clear that in the North American context visiting by elders is slipping away as a common practice except for pockets of close-knit communities. Those interviewed mentioned reasons for this such as the mobility of families so that relationships are slipping. Families no longer live locally so that elders don't know those they are visiting, or not very well. Except for the elderly and those ill, very few members of church families are home during the day. If they are, they prefer their privacy and don't want others to intrude in their time off. It is no longer accepted that elders or ministers simply drop by to visit a family.

---

4. Refer to the appendix for full details of those interviews.

Church members are often not home before 8pm to receive a traditional home visit and many regard such visits as an "invasion."

From the above it is clear that a big issue is how to build relationships. As one lecturer put it, accountability with a relationship equals caring. Accountability without a relationship equals judgment. It was admitted that many elders lack relational skills. Many are professional businessmen who are more used to making decisions and solving problems and feel quite inadequate in developing pastoral relationships. Elders seemed to be unaware that their primary task was faith formation and tended to react to problems. There is a need to look at the personal life of the elder and provide mentoring for his own spiritual development.

Concerns were expressed in relation to the eldership system such that they had too much to do. How can one interface pastoral care and discipleship such that the average elder can do it? Elders lack training and find that their first year in office is learning the role, the second is doing something and the third is thinking of getting out.

There was recognition that there was a need for new practices. It was said that Ephesians 4 was increasingly being used to develop the big picture; that pastoral care was about spiritual formation. There was a focus on small groups and on such concepts as household gatherings that were led by elders. There was the development of pastoral care teams and a division of labor between administrative elders and pastoral-care elders, depending on their gifting. There was a trend to see pastoral care in terms of discipleship and a greater need for discipling rather than discipline. There was a need to keep mentoring the new converts to ensure they keep growing spiritually. In all of this there was a real need for elders to be trained.

A look at this summary from the interview notes of the North American counterpart makes it clear there are trends of concern not only expressed by the participants of the focus groups in this research but far more broadly. It thus reinforces the conclusions of the focus group data and thus the need for this research to look for new ways of doing pastoral care by the elders.

5

An Overview of the Action Research

Introduction

IN THIS CHAPTER AN overview is given of the Action Research (AR) process as conducted by the elders' AR team. It takes the form of a narrative summary, giving the reader an experience of plausibility, seeing how the research evolved and how the AR team came to the position that emerged. The AR process is followed chronologically with an overview given of each AR team meeting.[1]

Action Research Team Meeting 1 (AR1)

The first AR team meeting, held on August 2, 2009, was organized through the researcher writing to the sessions of the Christian Reformed Churches in Classis NSW, inviting participation in the AR process and giving a brief summary of the research question and what the process entailed.

The AR Team

Seven elders responded to the invitation and attended the AR1 team meeting. The elders represented a good cross-section of the general eldership in the denomination: average age—56 years (range 43–74 years); average

---

1. Refer to the appendix on how to obtain all the extensive verbatim records, documents, and responses upon which this chapter is based.

time in the denomination—33 years (range 7–58 years); average years of experience as an elder—17 years (range 3–50 years); ethnic background—2 Australians, 1 South African, 4 Dutch; work experience—3 master's degree level professionals, 4 certificate level white collar/trades.

AR1 Resources

A set of eight resources was provided to the AR team members prior to the first meeting as reading assignments.[2]

AR1 Discussions/Conclusions

The AR team reviewed the doctoral research proposal document and the research question and agreed that it was a necessary issue for them to give their time.

INITIAL OBSERVATIONS

The team reviewed the focus group analysis and summary and accepted there were serious concerns with the current system of pastoral care. The results matched their own anecdotal observations.

NO STIPULATED METHOD

The team reviewed the New Testament and CRCA confessions and agreed that neither of these stipulated the method of the pastoral care provided by elders. It was recognized that the CRCA Church Order does specify that annual home visits are to be provided by elders. But the team was agreed that the Church Order does not hold the same authority as the Scriptures and confessions in the CRCA.

---

2. The documents included were: The Doctoral Research Proposal; The Research Question; Analysis of the Focus Groups; Summary of the Focus Group Analysis; Statement of Interview of CRCNA ministers; Review of New Testament and CRCA Confessions Re Task of Elders; Methodology Outline of the Action Research Process; Summary of How to Keep a Research Diary.

AR Method

The team was instructed in the AR method and they agreed that it was a good process with which they would work.

Cell Groups

As an initial way forward the AR team agreed that the focus for pastoral care in the CRCA churches should be the "cell groups." Elders could meet regularly with these groups and thus have oversight of the groups. It was determined that focus on the cell groups would assist to overcome the loss of community. As part of the spiritual oversight the elders would provide doctrinal supervision over the studies and discussions in the cell groups. The cell groups were seen as being self-ministering, allowing time for elders to do follow-up with individuals and dealing with special needs. This would assist with the "lack of time" issue. It was felt that elders could still do home visits with those families or individuals not attending cell groups.

Diaries for Observation

The team members were provided with diaries and instructed on how to keep an AR diary, noting such things as their thoughts, feelings, further ideas, as well as their observations of how they might experience trialing a new system.

Further Questions for Follow-up.

As part of the ongoing "planning" phase of the AR process, the team considered questions that needed further thought for the next AR team meeting. The questions included: What is pastoral care? What is the demarcation line between pastoral care provided by the cell group and that provided by the elders? How does an elder "supervise" a cell group? What does he look for? What skills are needed? Where does the elders' pastoral care role fit in with the proactive approach of "follow my example as I follow the example of Christ"? How committed are the elders? How inspired are they toward their roles? How well trained are they and how well versed in the Scriptures?

Action Research Team Meeting 2 (AR2)

The second AR team meeting was held on August 24, 2009.

AR2 Resources

A set of eight resources was provided to the AR team members prior to the second team meeting.[3]

AR2 Discussion and Conclusions

The team noted the conclusions of the AR1 team meeting and the resources provided and discussed the parameters of a plan to trial and observe.

Defining Small Groups

Initial discussion revolved around the need to clearly define what is required of the small groups. Part of the definition would be to take on board the need for the cell groups to align with the CRCA vision. It meant the cell groups could not just be about Bible study but should also include how the church members grow in the faith so that they would be able to share their faith.

Developing Relationships

It was pointed out that perhaps the real question was how to develop relationships. Many people in a small group do not really share with each other. If relationships were developed then when an issue arose church members could take it up personally with one another.

---

3. The documents included were: Elder A diary notes; Elder D diary notes; Elder F verbatim record of meeting/discussion with researcher; Researcher diary notes; Researcher notes of meeting with CRCA theological lecturer; Researcher doctoral paper: "Imaging God—To Be Human is to Be in Community"; Researcher doctoral paper: "Assessing the Model of Discipling by Jesus"; Researcher doctoral paper: "Program for Introducing a Mentoring Component in your Ministry."

Community and Spiritual Growth

The formation of relationships was seen as important in regards to the question: How does one grow spiritually? It involved an intellectual knowing of theology and the Bible. But there was also very much the need to be personal with one another, to be held accountable. It involved sharing a meal and coming to know and trust each other. The key would be relationships forming community. A diversity of things were needed to be considered to compensate for what was lost, for example, a larger group for socializing, small groups for spiritual growth and pastoral care, one-to-one relationships for mentoring.

Existing Groups

It was recognized that many existing Bible study and women's groups were doing more for each other in terms of pastoral care than was often recognized. It was seen as important to allow those existing groups to continue and for them to be encouraged to slowly change towards a more holistic approach as a growth group. Change could not be forced as previous experiences had made clear.

Sharing in Groups

A key issue in this change process was: how to foster genuine sharing and caring in small groups? Experience showed that many were restrained in sharing things even after being in groups for many years. There would be many who would be threatened by such openness. To assist with relationships and openness the groups would need, in addition to Bible study, the pastoral element, and also the social element. There was a need to see each other holistically.

Group Leaders and Elders

For the cell groups to go well they would need good leaders to drive them. Each group would have an elder to visit and oversee the group. The question was: Should the elder be the leader of the group given that elders were in office for three years? Because of this regular changeover of elders each small group would need a good leader to keep things going well. The elders could be partners with the group leaders.

Group Oversight

A key question was how would the elder do his overseeing in the group? Was it by shepherding, teaching, or observing? In the home visitation process, oversight was done by asking pointed questions of the family, for example, how is your spiritual life? How is your marriage? The elders could challenge, encourage, or exhort the family as required. How would the elder touch on those sorts of issues in the small group? Elders were not just to administer small groups. They needed to oversee the lives of their members and challenge them to growth. It would be helpful to have integrated studies: materials that focus on family issues, relational, or spiritual growth issues. It would require sensitivity on the part of the elder to bring up the practical issues in the Bible study.

Trust and Respect

Another key concern was how the elders were perceived: was there trust and respect for the elders? In the postmodern setting, trust would not be given simply because of the position a person held. Elders needed to earn trust. There was a need for the elder to develop the relationship with the group members and build trust in the small group. There was a need for elders to oversee "by being examples to the flock." The elder would demonstrate how others were to grow by the way he lived, his devotion to Scripture, and his prayer life. It was seen as important that the elder used Scripture to teach, encourage, or rebuke, because it was not his word that had authority but the Word of God.

Next Generation

It was recognized that the next generation would be expecting something different to the home visiting of the past. They were seen as culturally different, who communicate differently by means of texting, emails, Facebook, Twitter, and so on. The younger generation didn't just drop in for a chat, not only due to different relating styles, but also they appeared to have little free time.

Groups per Elder

Where there were more small groups than elders in a congregation it was suggested the elder may have at least two groups he would be responsible for. The elder could alternate between groups. If the groups meet fortnightly he would be in each group once per month. Given that the elder was providing oversight, not running the group, this could be manageable and sufficient.

Proactive Care

There was a need for elders not only to react to needs they observed in the small groups, but for them to proactively assist members to grow spiritually. Given there was such growth that would imply there would be less pastoral needs for the elder to deal with. And those members who had spiritually grown would then be in a position to further assist others. The elder could be teaching others, whether through the small groups or one to one. Such teaching would not necessitate academic training on the elder's part. It could involve modeling wisdom, a demonstration of humility and trust before God, a regular prayer life, and Bible reading. There needed to be intentionality about equipping others for leadership and also about raising the level of spiritual maturity with the resultant willingness to share the faith.

Caliber of Elders

The caliber of the elders was seen as below what was desired. It was argued that many of the structures of the previous generation had been lost. Church members were no longer doing family or personal devotions, little mentoring was provided through (extended) family, there was a general loss of Christian community. So these needed to be compensated for through training structures. There was a need to raise the spiritual level of the church members. That required that the elders' level of spiritual maturity should be raised first. This could be through mentoring as in the New Testament with Paul and Timothy. Elders needed to be more deliberate about it.

Focus on Pastoral Care

It was recognized that the workload of elders in session meetings was too much. Elders needed to be able to focus on pastoral care. Consideration was given to the practice of a sister denomination where elders were divided into those who had administrative and those who had pastoral roles. Given the small sessions in the CRCA the practicality of that was questioned. Also the CEO type model of church leadership was not deemed suitable, given the desire to see elders who disciple and train, not administer. The team identified a need for a total package to be considered including how session meetings were conducted so the elders could focus on their main calling.

Further Questions for Follow-up

At this point the AR team saw themselves in the planning phase of AR. A final model of pastoral care still needed to be developed but there was sufficient at this point to try out and observe. AR team members already participating in cell groups in their local churches could assume the role of the overseeing elder. They would observe the cell groups and consider questions like: What do they actually see happening in the cell group? What are the dynamics? What do they look for given they have oversight? These observations were to be diarized for the next AR team meeting.

Further questions for consideration included: What training was needed for the elder to fulfill this pastoral role in the cell group? Should the ministers disciple the elders? What should be done for those church members not involved in small groups? Would that be a role for retired elders? How would they tie in with session? What changes would be required for session as a whole so that elders could focus on their role of pastoral care?

Action Research Team Meeting 3 (AR3)

The third AR team meeting was held on October 12, 2009.

AR3 Resources

A set of four resources was provided for the AR team members prior to the team meeting.[4]

AR3 Discussion and Conclusions

The AR team reported on their observations in their small groups.

---

4. The resources included: Agenda for AR3 team meeting; Discussion points raised by AR2 team meeting; Elder A Diary notes; Elder E Diary notes.

Generational Preferences

One elder reported that older members predominantly preferred care by means of home visitation and the younger members preferred it by means of small groups.

Implications for the Small Group

Another elder reported that his small group was fairly optimistic about changing their group towards a more holistic approach. One of the implications they saw was that they would need to start earlier to make time for personal sharing. There was concern though that they were not used to being open with each other and that there would be a need to develop that openness. Such change would need to be done carefully because there was a tendency towards resistance.

Defining Growth Groups

It was observed that there is a need to define exactly the purpose of the small groups. A Bible study was quite different to a growth group. A growth group is what is needed: a holistic approach where members pray for each other, socialize, and bring non-Christian friends for outreach.

Some Suggestions

It was suggested that the small groups could follow the lead of the *Sticky Church*[5] book and discuss the Sunday sermons, unpacking the sermon for practical applications. There was also a need to move people along from "interested" to "total commitment" to "leaders."[6] Opportunities needed to be provided for missional activities for the members to practice what they are learning.

Caliber of Elders

The team observed that for the change to actually bear fruit there was a real need for elders of the "right material." It needed those with a real heart and commitment to the task. If that was not in place then there would be a

---

5. Osborne, *Sticky Church*.
6. Concepts found in Warren, *Purpose Driven Church*, 365–374.

real battle to attain the desired change. The AR team conceded from their experience it was hard to find the sort of talent required for good eldership. It was suggested that it was imperative to start looking at the younger men and to spend five to seven years developing those suitably gifted. The small groups could be a good place to look for and develop the upcoming leaders.

Further Planning

The researcher, to assist with further planning, introduced specific issues to focus the discussion on the practical outworking of the concepts being developed. The AR team agreed that the task of an elder was to (i) to defend and protect the "flock," (ii) to provide an example of Christian living, (iii) to teach/nurture/encourage/correct/disciple the members, and (iv) to be held accountable for the members of the church. To be able to do that the elders needed to assess and nurture (i) the member's faith, (ii) their spiritual growth, (iii) to oversee their life, work, marriage, family, and church life, (iv) and care for them in times of sickness and suffering. The AR team was encouraged to be very specific in terms of planning the practicalities of what the elder does with the small group. This included the need to oversee and observe, to consider how to encourage and challenge members, how to lead by example and to consider when a pastoral issue was dealt with by the small group and when it required the elders' attention by means of a personal visit. The question of the skills required for each of these aspects was also put to the team.

Elder's Role in Group

The AR team focused its planning on what the elder does in the small group and how it compared with what an elder does on an annual home visit. The assumption was made that the elder did not need to be leading the small group but could be a participant observer to fulfill his role. The elder, however, would need to be aware of the "observer effect" and that because of his presence church members could well be "on their best behavior." It was stipulated that the elder would need to become a natural, regular part of the group and not just come and observe occasionally. Irregular attendance would change substantially his role and influence in the group.

Elder's Gifting

It was recognized that the gifting of the individual elders varies, such that some would be very capable of leading the small group and other elders would not feel comfortable with that. The latter elder could be an example of quiet influence. It was suggested that the elder could influence the group discussions by offering suggestions or questions that would lead the conversation in an appropriate way. The elder could also set the example by sharing aspects of his life with the group.

Skills Required

In its planning the AR team considered the skills needed by the elder in his role on the small group.

Spiritual discernment: It was decided that the elder would need the ability of spiritual discernment. Such, of course, implied the elder was spiritually mature.

Modeling Christian behavior: The elder needed to model Christian behavior with the small group. This aspect was considered to be the distinct advantage of elders providing pastoral care via the small groups. The members could observe the life of the elder who could teach biblical truths, such as the need for wisdom and gentleness, by his example.

Bible knowledge: Good Bible knowledge was also essential to be able to encourage and challenge members. Any challenge or rebuke needed to be seen as what God said in his Word, a challenge that both the elder and members were to take to heart; and not a word of rebuke because the elder said so.

Mentoring: The elder needed to be able to provide mentoring and support for the small group leader. It was further recognized that elders needed relational and mentoring skills so the group members came to see and own for themselves what they needed to change in their lives for their own growth rather than being "told" by an authority figure.

Elder Training

It was recognized that there was a real need for elders to be continually trained and spiritually nurtured. It was seen as the task of the ministers to care for and equip the elders. The elders also needed to be intimate with the Bible, so that it deeply influenced their lifestyle.

Elder or Group Care

The team considered when a pastoral matter should be dealt with by the small group and when directly by the elder. It determined that the group could provide support, care, and prayer for each other in their various circumstances. Discipline type situations would require the elder to follow up with a home visit.

Action and Observation

The AR team agreed that the above was an outline of what it meant by an elder doing pastoral work in the small group. It was agreed to trial the plan in the small groups attended by the AR elders and to diarize their observations. In particular the team agreed to observe how they felt in their new role in the small groups, what worked for them, and how they assessed their skills. Of particular note was to observe if the small group they were attending was inclined towards purely studying the Bible and what the elder might do to try and encourage personal sharing, either by their own personal sharing or through the use of open questions.

Action Research Team Meeting 4 (AR4)

The fourth AR team meeting was held on November 16, 2009.

AR4 Resources

The AR team received eight resources from each other prior to the team meeting.[7]

---

7. The documents included: Agenda for AR4 team meeting; Discussion notes from the elder diaries; Assignment for the next meeting; Researcher diary notes; Elder A diary notes; Elder B diary notes; Elder E diary notes, Elder F diary notes.

AR4 Discussions and Conclusions

The AR team reviewed their diary notes, noting their observations on meetings with elders and small groups.

Low Caliber of Elders

The AR team acknowledged that the intent of the elders' oversight was to lead to spiritual formation. This required elders to lead by example, which also implied elders being held in respect. But it was observed that such was often not the case and a reason for this poor respect towards the elders and low home visiting rates was attributed to the caliber of many elders. It was expressed that the heart of the elders was not always where it ought to be. Though seen as a generalization it was felt that the average elder was not really committed and had a serious lack of understanding as to what it meant to be an elder.

Elder Training

It was observed that some elders had assumed that life experience and a personal walk with God was sufficient preparation for eldership and if called to the eldership then they should be ready. The team reflected that while God calls to office, the session was still responsible to test those nominated for a real relationship with God, a godly character, and then to provide training for the competencies required. A crucial point for the elder's development was relationship building. This was needed to develop respect and trust and thus the confidence for members to share pastoral concerns with an elder. A key to developing openness was for the elder to be open with his parishioners.

Elders Mentored

An important aspect of the elders' training would be for the minister to mentor his elders. Such mentoring would then assist the elder in his role as mentor. It was suggested that members tended to struggle not with being overseen and held accountable, but with the method or manner in which that was conducted. Having a "spiritual friend" would be highly desirable.

Elder Accountability

It was admitted that elders could be lax in the new system. If the elder was not proactive, underlying problems would go undetected or if detected not followed up. An accountability system was needed for the elders.

Elder's Focus

It was observed that it was important to know where the elder should focus because session work could involve so many things. It was determined that the crux of the elder's role is overseeing the flock, which included discipling, pastoral care, and growing the church members so they were assisted to mature in Christ. An elder's "performance" should be measured by what he is really accountable for.

Role of the Minister

It was recognized as an implication of the elders being held accountable by the minister, that the minister could not do the bulk of the pastoral work. Such would take him away from mentoring his elders. The question was raised: What if the minister did not feel competent to train his elders? Should some one be appointed by classis or the denominational theological college to train elders? There was a need to develop the DNA of the local church such that training for leadership was a natural part of what happened at the church.

Elder's Questions in Small Groups

One observation gave consideration as to whether the types of questions asked by elders at a home visit could be included in the small group discussion without alerting members they were being "grilled." It was determined it would be easier if the small group was aware of the elder's role to look after pastoral and doctrinal issues in the group and as such the group would be comfortable with that.

Recalling Group Conversation

It was also noted that it was difficult to recall who said what in discussions, hampering possible follow-up.

Elder Preparation

There was also the need to recognize that an elder could no longer sit back and relax in the small group. The elder now needed to be well prepared beforehand and looking for opportunities to ask suitable questions. It was suggested the elder could pass on questions to the small group leader to incorporate into the discussions.

Deflecting Questions

It was pointed out that it was important for an elder not to provide all the answers in the group discussions. The elder needed to develop the skills of deflecting questions so the group members worked out their own responses and applied the teaching for themselves.

Follow-up Action and Observation

The AR team agreed to continue road testing their role in the small groups. The focus would be on the elders diarizing internal issues such as: How am I coping? What skills do I need?

Assigned Questions

The researcher tabled a set of questions dealing with practical issues for the elder in the small group. For example: What is the observer effect of the elder on the small group if his mindset, age or gender differed from the small group participants? Should the elder's role be a proactive leader or an observer; a listener or a teacher? Several questions relating to developing trust were listed, as well as the effect of an elder following up on what was shared in the small group; would it tend to impact on further sharing? There were also questions on the skills needed by an elder in the small group such as listening, emotional intelligence, and questioning skills.

Care for Those not in Groups

It was agreed that the team would give consideration to those who were not in small groups. If home visits were to be given for all those people, would the effect be a doubling up of what elders are required to do, namely small groups and also home visits?

Defining Spiritual Growth

Given that it was agreed that the elder's job was to nurture spiritual growth it was decided to give thought to how an elder could do that and also to consider what the factors were that created spiritual growth.

Action Research Team Meeting 5 (AR5)

The fifth AR team meeting was held on December 14, 2009.

AR5 Resources

The AR team received seven resources from each other prior to the team meeting.[8]

AR5 Discussions and Conclusions

The AR team discussed what they had achieved in terms of "road testing" their proposed system of overseeing the members by means of the small groups.

Elder's Self Awareness

An opening observation was in relation to the elder's self-awareness. How well did the elders know themselves, their own motivations? What really was their agenda as they visited others? Were they aware of how that impacted what they brought to the visit?

Need for Adjustment

It was observed that the new approach would take some getting used to. The elder now needed to be more alert, observing and discerning what was happening in the lives of the church members. This was not easy given that on the whole small group members tend to be reserved.

---

8. Documents included: Paper—Concepts on Spiritual Growth; Elder A diary notes; Elder B diary notes; Elder C diary notes; Elder D diary notes; Elder E diary notes; Elder F diary notes.

Not Policing

Care needed to be taken that the elder's role in the small group didn't itself again become perceived as "policing." Elders would need to report on the group to the session and it was expressed that those comments could "leak" back to the small group. So elders needed to be upfront about why they were in the small group. It would need time to develop the trust and a certain spiritual maturity of the group members to receive that oversight. Elders would need to develop genuine relationships and not try to micromanage, watching every move.

Elder's Focus

The focus for the elders should be about teaching the Word, modeling faith, and enjoying and growing together through community. The focus was to be spiritual growth, which came through seriously looking at God's Word and together communally loving and inspiring each other to follow that Word. It was recognized that the elder would be working over time to try and connect what was being studied to how it could lead to spiritual growth and how he could contribute to help that occur. But pushing too hard could be counter-productive, so it could be better at times to mentor group members individually.

Reticence to Change

It was observed that people would be defensive about any change, which included being more open with each other, especially in the presence of the elder. The elders would need to work in a very humble, servant-like way.

Those not in Small Groups

The AR team reflected on ways for providing pastoral care for those not in small groups. It was estimated that in certain congregations up to fifty percent of the church members would not be in small groups, including the elderly and those not interested. Should elders be required to have their own small groups and also home visit those not in small groups? Would that not imply a doubling up of their work? Several approaches were suggested:

Technology: Elders needed to work smarter and use the technology and various forms of communication to be in contact with people.

Session structure: The way session was structured could be different such that elders were allocated certain roles, some to small groups and others to caring for those not in small groups. It would not be appropriate to have all elders do small groups and home visitations.

Elderly: It was recognized that visits with the elderly would not necessarily need to look for spiritual growth because little of that would be occurring at their age. They needed to be affirmed in their faith at the moment of the visitation.

Retired elders: It was suggested that elders retired from session could be involved in pastoral care. Such a suggestion implied the recognition that a person did not stop being an elder when he finished his three-year term in office. He should still be seen as a role model and pastoral care could be done by these men.

Care by others: Pastoral care could be done by others besides the elders. Volunteers could have four or five families to visit and could refer matters of concern to the elders in session.

The AR team saw it as legitimate to involve others in the pastoral care of those not in small groups because the elders' role was to oversee, not do it all. That oversight was essential to hold each other and others accountable.

Accountability

The team observed that much depends on the enthusiasm of the persons involved in providing pastoral care. In reality not all the elders and pastoral carers would be doing what they had been assigned to do. Thus an accountability structure needed to be put in place otherwise much would still be left undone.

It was stated that it was the minister's role to hold the elders and other pastoral carers accountable. Ministers could then also identify specific gaps in the training and provide follow-up training after the initial training of the elders and pastoral care workers.

Balance of Minister's Role

A practical concern was raised if the minister did a lot of mentoring with the elders and the pastoral carers: it implied he would not be available to do all the pastoral care himself. This was still the expectation in many congregations. Finding the balance in this would be critical. When was it essential for the minister to visit, when for two elders, and when was it appropriate for a pastoral carer? This would need to be defined so the congregation understood and accepted it. People might complain that they had not really been visited unless the minister had been to see them.

To help assist in the balance of expectations and time management it was suggested that the minister should not try to mentor the individual elders and pastoral-care workers, but rather hold team meetings. But even then it was suggested that there would still be a need for some one-to-one meetings. It was observed the elders or pastoral carers could claim all was going well at such meetings but not really doing what was required.

Female Carers

A question was raised as to whether the AR team envisaged problems with having female pastoral carers. While it was recognized that certain congregations in the denomination would object, the team saw it as being legitimate because such carers did not have oversight but would be providing general care and feeding back to the elders.

The female pastoral carers would be encouraged to read the Bible and pray with members being visited. This was seen as being essential to a pastoral visit, which was not just a social visit. And as any Christian could read the Bible and pray with another person it was not seen as crossing over to the elders' role of oversight.

Spiritual Growth Matrix

The AR team reviewed a paper presented by the researcher entitled "Concepts on Spiritual Growth." The document listed four stages of spiritual growth as well as four categories of spiritual catalysts that could be involved in moving a person to the next stage of growth. The AR team considered the document to be a useful summary of spiritual growth. They saw it as valid to use the matrix as a tool to observe and define where members of the small groups might be in their own spiritual growth. It was suggested the matrix could be used with the small group to stimulate thinking about the member's own individual spiritual journey and to convince them of the need for the small group to change into a holistic growth group. For an individual's growth it was considered it would be good for the elder to have one-on-one discussions using the matrix as an assessment tool.

Mentor Training

The suggestion of elders providing mentoring raised the question as to how they could do that if they had never experienced being mentored themselves. The issue of the elder's personal spiritual growth was seen as vital, since an elder could not bring another person beyond his own spiritual maturity level. Sessions could inadvertently hold back their congregations because the elder's own personal growth had been stymied and they hadn't been mentored.

So the question was put: What, practically, was needed to raise the bar for the elders? It was suggested that either the minister of the local church mentors his elders or some one from outside the congregation might do that.

Nominations for Elders

It was pointed out that the spiritual maturity and gifting of the potential elder at the nomination stage for office was very important. It could not simply be assumed that if the elder had been nominated and called by means of the congregation's vote, that everything was fine. There needed to be serious thought given to the criteria used to consider a man for nomination, beyond what at times were simply social skills and popularity in the congregation. The difficulty was when people in a congregation did not know each other well it was hard to ascertain whether a given person qualified as an elder. It was stated that the small groups would be an excellent place for elders to observe potential office bearers in terms of their spiritual maturity, character, and competencies.

Generating Change

The AR team discussed the issue of how the training for elders and the changes to pastoral care could actually be set up. What was needed to generate the change required? It was suggested that someone with a certain "authority" would be required. It needed to come from the denomination's theological college or the classis. Just trying to change and provide training locally would not be readily accepted.

The congregations would need to have a complete package, including the realization of the need for change and then training tools for it to happen. It would be appropriate to have a report going to the churches and then to have classis training days to put the issue on the agenda of the churches for discussion. It would then be important for local churches to try out the new ideas.

Some form of structure needed to be developed as the changes and training required would take time. The continual change of elders each year as they completed their term in office made an ongoing approach essential. What was required was a person to drive the program, focusing first on the ministers and assisting them with the training of their elders.

It was noted that the denominations using the Westminster Confession as their basis were more proactive in training their elders. Several denominations in the USA had set up an "elders' institute." It was noted that their training focused on instruction in the confession and doctrines and less on practical pastoral training.

Follow-up Action and Observation

It was agreed that the AR team would continue to "road test" elders' pastoral care via small groups using the same questions that had been put to the team prior to this AR team meeting. It was deemed that these were the "nuts and bolts" questions because they were the practical issues that came up.

Action Research Team Meeting 6 (AR6)

The sixth AR team meeting was held on February 8, 2010.

AR6 Resources

Two resources were supplied to the AR team members by the researcher.[9]

Discussion and Conclusions

The main item for discussion at this team meeting was the "Interim Report to the Sessions." The researcher wrote a position paper incorporating the conclusions of the team from the previous team meetings.

---

9. Documents include: Agenda for AR6 Team Meeting; Interim Report to the Sessions.

Broader Review

It was decided to send the "Interim Report" to the individual elders in each CRCA congregation in NSW to validate the findings of the AR team. The elders would be asked to give their personal reflections on the report and to consider the practicalities of the proposals. It was deemed that at the current stage the report and its review remained an academic exercise, part of the AR process. Once the AR was completed and the dissertation was written, then the material can be officially presented to classis. It was acknowledged that in the interim any church was welcome to trial the conclusions in the "Interim Report" if they are so inclined.

It was decided that the researcher would visit a number of sessions to discuss the report. It was acknowledged that many elders would struggle to read the report and really appreciate the issues without the researcher to elaborate on the report. It was also recognized that the elders receiving the "Interim Report" could be quite challenged, even threatened, given that the AR team had expressed their serious concern about the caliber of many elders. It was also decided that several senior ministers around the denomination would receive the "Interim Report."

Assessing the "Interim Report"

The AR team spent much of its time working through the "Interim Report" assessing the various sections and making amendments where it was deemed necessary. The team was satisfied that the paper addressed the various issues and questions that the elders had.

Clarifying Pastoral Partnering

The team spent time discussing the section "Pastoral Care for Those not in Small Groups." The paper suggested as one option a Pastoral Partnering Program (PPP) in which pastoral care workers, deacons, and retired elders could assist the elders in session. The team clarified that pastoral care workers, and the other carers should meet together regularly and thus report to the elders on session at such team meetings.

It was decided that initial training for those in the PPP should be given by the minister of the congregation and that ongoing training should be part of the regular team meetings. This ongoing training could be given by the elders who would have their own group of pastoral care workers, deacons, and retired elders as their pastoral team within the PPP. If the elders were not suitably equipped to provide that training the minister would need to provide such training at each team meeting.

It was deemed imperative that the minister mentors his elders and holds them (and their team) accountable to actually do their task. No matter what system was devised, if those involved were not maintaining their duties the work would fail.

A further practical concern was that various ministers might not feel competent or compelled to train their elders, especially if the minister was young and inexperienced. In such a case ministers could feel intimidated by elders many years their senior, with 20–30 years of church leadership experience.

The team determined that the focus group research indicated that elders were not doing their ministry well so both the minister and the elders would need to be trained together. The team further concluded that it might be necessary for the classis to provide training from outside the local congregation.

Follow-up Action and Observation

Apart from sending the "Interim Report" to the elders of the various churches in NSW, the AR team decided to continue observing how they functioned as elders in their small groups.

In particular it was decided to trial the spiritual growth matrix and determine how useful it would be to identify where small group members might be on the spiritual growth continuum. The AR team were encouraged to diarize their thoughts concerning how the elder would go about determining the spiritual level of small group members, how long it took, what the effect on the small group might be if the members were at different levels, and how the elder might provide ways for the members to grow.

The other item to diarize was for the elders to consider how they might be "examples" of Christ to the group. How would they need to speak and act? How well were they actually doing; were they being real or playing a role? What would that say about their own spiritual growth and where did they need to grow themselves?

Action Research Team Meeting 7 (AR7)

The seventh AR team meeting was held on March 29, 2010.

AR7 Resources

Two resources were made available to the AR team by the researcher.[10]

Discussion and Conclusions

The focus of the AR7 team meeting was to review the responses by the elders and ministers to the "Interim Report." The researcher collated the responses from individual elders and ministers as well as from the verbatim record of two focus groups with local church sessions. A summary was made of the collation, which formed the AR team agenda. The team spent the major part of its time responding to each of these agenda items.

THE RESEARCH QUESTION

The overall response to the "Interim Report" was positive. The team noted there were those who expressed they were at odds with the team's conclusions.

No predetermined results: Elders from one church questioned whether the research had been led to a predetermined result. The AR team was adamant that the proposed method of pastoral care was their own work and had not been pushed in any particular direction by the researcher as inspection of the verbatim record would make clear.

No disenfranchisement: The team also rejected the misconception that the proposed approach would disenfranchise those churches which preferred to remain with the traditional home visitation. The approach used in any particular church was at the discretion of the local elders. However, where the home visiting system was not working, it was deemed that the AR team's proposal provided a valid and viable alternative.

Purpose of pastoral care: A further criticism was that the effectiveness of a method of pastoral care could not be determined unless the purpose was clear. One response put forward the view that pastoral care was not the

---

10. The documents included: Collation of Responses/Critique to the Interim Report and a Summary of Responses/Agenda for the AR7 Team Meeting. Further documents providing the background research to the Collation of Responses are the Letter to the Ministers/Elders, Individual Responses/Critique to Interim Report, Verbatim of Session A Focus Group/Critique Interim Report and Verbatim of Session B Focus Group/Critique Interim Report.

primary work of the elders, but rather the equipping and empowering of the church members. The team responded that the key scriptural idea for the elders was "oversight." The point of the elders having oversight was to ensure members were growing spiritually. That purpose was clearly articulated in the AR team's work and report. It was further clarified that "oversight" should not be seen in terms of "policing." A better analogy would be "project management," ensuring there were Bible studies, pastoral care, training, and evangelism—a holistic approach to ensure the growth of members.

Function/form: Another criticism was that there was a need to better define the "function/form" distinction in pastoral care. It was perceived that the AR team had provided another "form" of pastoral care, which could itself be restrictive. What was needed was to define the "function" of pastoral care as described in the Bible and to provide a variety of "forms" that would be suitable for the congregations in their particular circumstances.

The AR team acknowledged that different "forms" may be needed. What the AR team's work demonstrated was precisely that: discerning the "function" of pastoral care and demonstrating the validity of a different "form." The AR proposal provided something concrete, a practically viable approach that took into account the particular circumstances identified through the focus groups.

The AR team determined that what it was putting forward was an alternative, not the only "form" that could be considered valid. The team noted that there needed to be room for various "forms." The responses made clear that some churches would be threatened by the suggested changes, especially since the traditional "form" worked for them and they saw no need of change. On the other hand, other churches had already moved beyond what the AR team was advocating because their situation was quite different.

The main "function" of the elders was summarized as having spiritual oversight that ensured holistic care for members such that they grew spiritually, were empowered to use their gifts, and reached out with the gospel.

The Need for Change

The responses under this category revealed two directions: those who didn't see a need for change and those who did.

Against change: Those against change reaffirmed the traditional home visiting system because it worked very well in their congregation. The AR team did not deny this and reiterated that it put forward its proposal as a viable alternative in settings where the home visiting system did not work.

Negative remarks towards focus group members for expressing concern about the current system were deemed unfair. The remarks may have occurred because of misconceptions about focus group participants, the assumption being that dissident church members tended to be involved in focus groups. The reality was most of the focus group participants were long-term committed senior members of the congregations and elders.

The team accepted the comment that numerous home visits were simply poor visits without necessarily implying that the system was invalid. But it argued that, even accepting the current system, such poor visits demonstrated the need for training for elders.

The team expressed some consternation at the responses indicating ministers were incapable of training elders and considered some ways of remedying that, such as the denominational theological college providing education for that or even for ministers to obtaining a Certificate IV in coaching or training through a local training college.

For change: The responses that recognized a need for change noted that the focus group results were not surprising. Such feedback was widespread and the need for fresh thinking was great. The new generations were seen to think very differently and needed to be approached differently. The AR team accepted that what was required at a local level could vary greatly depending on the particular circumstances of the congregation.

The responses advocating change also indicated what the change needed to be. There was a need for elders to focus on discipling and leading by example, preparing the church members for ministry and maturing in the faith. The AR team agreed, since these things came through in the focus group results and were the key areas of their own AR results. The focus on elders doing their pastoral care through small groups was to provide community so that they could "model" the faith and "lead by example."

It was acknowledged that there were churches which had far more small groups than they had elders. It became clear that small-group leaders would need to take a leading role in pastoral care and would need to be trained with the elders and work closely with them. With such training and experience in the small group, the group leader would be well prepared for taking an elder's role in due course.

It was also seen as important to reiterate the "one another" passages in the New Testament. Pastoral care was what church members did for each other.

A Suggested Way Forward: Growth Groups

The AR team interacted with numerous comments.

Balanced view: The AR team concurred with the comment that growth groups were greatly needed and provided the opportunity to relate with members regularly. This provided a more balanced view of their spiritual life than a once-per-year home visit.

DNA of the church: The team also accepted the notion that growth groups should be part of the DNA of the church, the engine room to stimulate spiritual growth, training and outreach. The team accepted the caution that growth groups should not simply focus on the care and growth of the members in the group but should also be the means for outreach.

Ongoing strategy: It was also accepted that if the growth groups were to be effective there needed to be an ongoing strategy to maintain and multiply the groups. It was commented that there were plenty of resources for setting up and developing a small group program and that the focus of the AR was more on what elders did in the small groups.

Not in small groups: A comment was noted that only half of a congregation might be in small groups implying others would miss out on pastoral care. The team reiterated that the "Interim Report" had a section on those not in small groups, for example, having a pastoral partnering program. It was noted that one respondent suggested that the small groups could adopt the families not in a small group and provide care for them. That would assist in reducing the elders' workload in visiting such families.

Levels of care: The team acknowledged as valid the comment that it was not easy to produce good levels of care in growth groups. Members were very busy and were often reticent to being open about their lives. That was a reason for the AR team's emphasis on elders modeling openness in the groups and developing skills in reflective listening and asking open questions. It was deemed important that the people participating in the small groups became familiar with the proposed system so they didn't feel their privacy was being invaded.

Group leaders: The team also accepted the comment that there would be an increased expectation on small-group leaders in terms of preparing for the Bible study, being trained, and so forth. If the defining of the group leader's role and their training was not done well the lynchpin of the approach would be missing. The team agreed that training was essential, but local ministers might need assistance in that.

Elders' Oversight of Growth Groups

The AR team noted that none of the responses indicated anything against the concept of elders fulfilling their role of spiritual oversight via growth groups.

Number of groups per elder: Responses related to practicalities such as whether an elder looking after two groups (or more) was too much given the other session and committee roles the elders had. The AR team considered that no elder should have more than two growth groups and that having two groups was achievable. This was assuming the groups meet fortnightly and the elder was prepared to go out one night a week for the small group and another for other session work. This had been the workload under the previous system. But it was conceded that, given the current circumstances, this might be too much for many elders.

Local circumstances: It was also clear that considerations on how things were structured depended very much on the size of the congregation, the number of gifted people that were available, and so forth.

Use of group leaders: Where there were a limited number of elders, especially in larger congregations, consideration should be given to greater use of small-group leaders assisting the elders. It was felt that members would be happier to run a small group and care for those people than to take on the office of elder with all the responsibilities that went with it.

Mentoring: The concern that mentoring was difficult or foreign for many men was seen by the team as a fact of life, but it needed to be encouraged if elders were to help others grow spiritually.

Variety of roles: The team also accepted the comment that there should be a variety of roles for elders in the session depending on their individual gifting.

Pastoral Care for Those not in Small Groups

The team noted that the responses were generally supportive.

Training trainers: The team took on board the concern that ministers could be so tied up with training elders and pastoral care workers that they would be exhausted by it. It was important for ministers to train trainers.

Pastoral Care Definition

The AR team accepted the criticism that the definition of pastoral care in the "Interim Report" was too narrow, though it is the standard definition in many pastoral care textbooks. The definition needed to be more organic, for example, that of "shepherding" including feeding, leading, protecting, and caring. It involved the goal of Christ-like maturity and included discipling, equipping, and training.

Training of Elders

The AR team agreed with all the responses to this section of the "Interim Report."

Training: Training in the role of elder was vital; without it elders floundered and were set up to fail. Training needed to be done prior to ordination otherwise there would be insufficient time available. Training should not just be "official" classes but should also include one-on-one mentoring.

Small groups: The small groups should be seen as "leadership farms": places to identify potential elders. Elders could be role models of eldership in the small groups, demonstrating what eldership was about.

Skills: Elders should not be seen as having a "mortgage on knowledge" but should be taught that through listening and good questions they could assist church members to arrive at the answers for themselves and live by those principles. There was a need to teach the importance of prayer as a major part of the elder's life.

Home: The first base for discipling and growing young men for leadership began in the home. Elders should encourage that and not try to provide all the training.

Implications for Sessions/Church Councils

The AR team noted there was general agreement from the responses for the need to prioritize pastoral care at session meetings.

It was noted that elders could be distracted by committee work as there was a tendency for them to be problem solvers and decision makers rather than carers and disciple makers.

The team accepted the caution that session work was more than pastoral care for church members. Oversight of the missional dimension was part of their role as well. The priority of prayer was also acknowledged.

Implications for Ministers

The AR team noted the responses to the "Interim Report" in general which conceded that ministers needed to be training their elders.

There was a concern that the report implied ministers should not be involved in pastoral care themselves but were to train others to do it. The team determined that what was needed was a balanced approach between the minister's involvement in pastoral care and training. Ministers definitely needed to be involved in pastoral care, especially with critical issues. They also needed to model how it was to be done. The team discerned a tendency for ministers to overly hold onto one role, presumably because they were good at it (pastoral care) and to forgo another role because they were not experienced or trained in it (training elders).

The team determined that the local minister needed to equip church members to take over certain aspects of ministry, especially in a one-minister church, and that he needed to prioritize that point. The team recognized they could expect resistance on this point from ministers. A possibility is that an experienced elder could provide training and so take some of the load off the minister.

Implications for Classis

The AR team noted the responses to this section of the "Interim Report."

No approval needed: There were responses that questioned the need for the AR team proposals to go to classis or synod for approval. The different views in the denomination implied ongoing debate and that approval would only be held up. Numerous congregations were already well into implementing other new strategies so approval was not needed. Official adoption of a new system could be interpreted that it was the only way pastoral care should be done. That system itself would eventually need to be changed. The AR team concurred with this reasoning and decided that it was up to the local congregations to determine how they would react to their proposals.

Dissemination: The team's findings could be disseminated through the denominational magazine, outlining the rational for an alternative model. It could also be emailed to local ministers and church sessions. It was also suggested that training should be set up to carefully explain the elements of the AR team's proposals and trial it in the local congregations.

Elders' Institute: The team reviewed the responses suggesting the implementation of an "elder's institute" and the need for classis or synod to appoint a person to train elders. The AR team agreed that training was required, but deemed it not feasible to have one person provide such training across the whole of Australia. An online course by the denomination's theological college was seen as having value, but only in terms of providing theological background knowledge. Practical training was seen as necessary which would be done best by means of practical exercises in the local church and by mentoring.

Conclusion

The AR team came to the conclusion that its work was completed. It was now up to the researcher to take on board the team's resolutions concerning the responses to the "Interim Report," much of which validated the team's proposals and helped clarify the issues. The AR team was keen to see its work go to the churches and not just be seen as an academic exercise. The researcher was encouraged to provide training for local churches so that the material would be given a hearing and trialed.

6

Conclusions

Introduction

THE PURPOSE OF THIS research was to establish a pastoral care method by the elders of the Christian Reformed Churches of Australia (CRCA) relevant to the circumstances of twenty-first-century Australia.

Research Question

The research question hypothesized that the existing method of pastoral care by the elders in the CRCA, that of home visitation, was losing its effectiveness.

Literature Search

The literature search, while demonstrating the purpose and value of the home visiting system, confirmed the potential of the concerns.

Focus groups

The consistent results across all eight focus groups, the broader denominational consultation, and the international comparison established that concerns about the home visiting by elders were valid.

Places of Effectiveness

In the international comparison it was stated that in the North American context visiting by elders was slipping away as a common practice, except for pockets of close-knit communities. This is significant. It implies that where the original conditions prevail—that is, a close church community in a conservative setting—the home visiting system can still function well. So despite the various concerns raised by the focus groups, there will be certain congregations where the home visits by elders are done well.

Key Issues

What is significant about the key issues raised by the focus groups is their similarity to those in the literature search and the fact that they were raised spontaneously in response to an open question about the experience of those who had received or conducted a home visit.

Little Prior Relationships

Often members were visited by those they didn't really know, who would ask them personal questions about their faith. The frequency of the visits varied. But even the required annual visits were not sufficient to build a relationship to be able to confide in an elder.

Training Required

There was a need for training the elders. The elders were seen as meaning well but not doing the task that was really required. Elders were described as being voted in and thrown in the deep end.

A Routine

A lot of the visits were described as a formal process, going through the routine and "ticking the boxes." Numerous participants, including elders referred to the visits as "policing."

Generational Differences

Concerns were expressed that the younger generation found they had little in common with the older elders. The older generation accepted and desired to have home visits with the younger generation but the younger generation tended to think differently and expected something different.

Suggested Alternatives

The focus groups concluded that the New Testament did not give a clear "how to" in terms of a method for pastoral care by the elders, but focused more on the character of the elder. The elder was to be a role model for those in his care. Pastoral care was also seen as what church members did for each other, especially through small groups.

A new approach should include elders providing mentoring and leading by example, as well as having small groups and pastoral teams. It was also expressed that elders needed to provide opportunities for involvement in missions and ministry. For that, the elders needed training. A discipling process would be the best way to train the elders.

Action Research

This research had seven elders devise such a new approach by means of the Action Research (AR) method over a six-month period. These are their conclusions:

Small Groups

It was decided to focus on elders providing pastoral care through small groups to compensate for the lack of meaningful relationships between the elders and the church members. It was also decided that since the spiritual growth of the church members was the purpose for the elders' pastoral care, that small groups have been shown to be the best medium to assist with that aim.

Holistic Groups

In particular it was important to have holistic growth groups and not just Bible studies. Holistic groups would include worship, mutual pastoral care and support, including holding each other accountable. They would also involve social and family activities, identifying and using spiritual gifts, reaching out to family and friends, as well as identifying and developing new leaders.

Elders Partnering with Group Leaders

For the elders to provide oversight and pastoral care through the small groups the elders would need to cooperate and partner with the small-group leaders. The group leaders could maintain consistency as the elders had a three-year term. The elders would be participants and observers in the groups. While some elders would be gifted to lead the group others were not so gifted. So the focus would be on the elders being participants in the full life of the group. In that role they would be able to observe and oversee the group. With good listening skills and discernment the elder would know the real needs and issues of the members, including their level of spiritual development.

Group Leaders

The group leaders were recognized as essential in the new approach and would need to receive appropriate training. It was also recognized that where there was a limited number of elders the group leaders could be assistants to the elders. Many would prefer the group-leader role because of the greater responsibilities the elders have.

Elders Building Trust

In the small group the elder would need to focus on developing relationships with the group members. Trust and respect needed to be earned. The "observer effect" of the elder could hinder openness in the group.

Elders Modeling Openness

It was recognized that many people in the CRCA small groups tended to be reserved even after years of being together. So there is a need for the elder in the group to assist genuine sharing by his own example. His role was not to be seen as policing the group; it was not about controlling outward behavior, but modeling behavior.

Elders Teaching for Spiritual Growth

The elder would need to see that his role in the group was one of teaching towards spiritual growth. Such should not necessarily be seen in terms of theological knowledge but more in terms of their own life example, being a model of a mature Christian, or at least a fellow traveler a bit further along the road able to bring some form of practical Christian example.

Practical Application

Elders needed to give consideration to the practical application of the Bible studies such that group members were encouraged to make practical changes in their lives. The elder might provide a set of additional questions for the group leader. The elder could give consideration to how the questions asked at traditional home visits might be included in the small group at appropriate points. Elders should make use of "open questions" to help facilitate open sharing. Elders should not attempt to provide answers to the issues but deflect questions such that the group members find their own answers and are empowered to take greater ownership for their spiritual growth.

God's Word

Whatever guidance an elder did give should be that which the Bible provided and not just his ideas. The elder should recognize that whatever authority he had was that of Jesus and his Word.

Elders Discerning Spiritual Level

It is important for the elder to discern the level of spiritual growth of the group members and consider ways to initiate catalysts to promote spiritual growth. A matrix provided for the AR team was considered one way of discerning the spiritual level.

Elders and Group Care

The elder would need to assist the small-group members to pastorally nurture and care for each other. The elder would need to give guidance in discerning when a pastoral matter should be dealt with by the small group and when by the elder or session. Certainly the group would be involved in providing support, accountability, and prayer. Where necessary the elder would follow up personally where they discerned matters that required more than the group could do for each other.

Discerning Potential Leaders

Elders should also be aware of those in their small group as to who would make potential leaders. Together with the small group leader the elder could arrange for one-on-one mentoring and help develop long-term training.

Elders With Two Groups

The elders may need to be involved with more than one small group, though many of the respondents were wary of such, given the other responsibilities of the elder. In whatever is decided in the local church setting, it is imperative that the elder becomes a regular and natural part of the group. Otherwise his role will be compromised.

Care for Those not in Groups

The AR recognized that a significant proportion of a congregation might not be involved in the small groups. It was decided that to ask elders to be involved in the small groups and also provide home visits for those not in small groups would be doubling the work of the elder and losing the gains in the new approach.

Using Pastoral Carers

It was deemed legitimate to involve others to visit those not in small groups involving elders retired from office and female pastoral carers. It was argued that while elders have the responsibility of oversight it did not mean they needed to do all the pastoral care. Whoever would assist with pastoral care would be accountable to the elders. It was also accepted that small groups could assist by caring for those not in small groups.

Pastoral Partnering

One model detailed by the AR involved a pastoral partnering program (PPP) where retired elders, deacons, and pastoral carers would be assigned three to five families with whom they had rapport. These pastoral partners would be contacted every three to four weeks by means of the various methods of communication or visited at home. The PPP team would meet every two months for general reporting, training, and prayer.

Accountability

Whatever form the care for those not in small groups would take, it was important to have a system of accountability. Not all elders and alternate carers would be following up on their assigned members as required. They would need ongoing encouragement and mentoring.

Elders Need Training

The AR team determined there was a serious deficit in the caliber of many elders and in the training for their role.

Compensating What Was Lost

There was a need to compensate for what was no longer there; such as the close-knit village in a Christian community where important roles such as that of elders could be learned by observation. There was little being done in the way of family devotions that modeled a spiritual life by the father of the family. There was little in the way of the extended family or community providing natural mentoring due to the mobility of families and scattered suburban living. So there needed to be an intentionality to model eldership, in such a way that it invoked trust and respect and inspired others to seek office (1 Tim 3:1).

What is Needed

There was a need to find the right material in terms of the character and gifting of potential elders. There was a need to consider criteria for nominations and sessions needed to test those nominated.

Small groups could be seen as "leadership farms" to identify and observe potential elders. The elder in the small group could model the role of the elder as had been done previously in the village. The elder and small group could observe in a potential elder his spiritual maturity, character, and competencies.

There was a need for sessions to provide support for families in terms of the upbringing of their children in the faith. It was argued that nurturing for eldership should start in the home. Young men with potential should be mentored for a number of years.

Training for eldership should be done prior to ordination. Elders were far too busy once in office to do serious training. But without prior training too many elders were floundering.

Focus of Training

Training for elders would first need to focus on the character of the elder and his relationship with his Lord. Given that the goal of pastoral care is not to "police" but to encourage the members toward spiritual maturity then the elders themselves needed to be examples of that maturity in Christ. Ministry derives from the elder's relationship with Jesus whom the elder represents.

Not Solving Problems

Ministry is not just a matter of learning a technique or quoting the appropriate Bible passages. Nor is the elder's ministry about solving problems. Many elders as businessmen or tradesmen are used to "fixing" things. The elders need to understand that they minister through listening and providing input from God's Word. The church member then is to respond in faith to Jesus, to be accountable for their own actions, to resolve their own issues via prayer, the Word and the Spirit.

Elders' Need to be Mentored

The best place for training elders would be by means of mentoring from the minister. His first pastoral responsibility should be the spiritual growth of the elders. Training should not just involve classes or readings but involve a genuine discipling and apprenticeship approach.

Devotional Life

The mentoring would include ensuring a good devotional life by the elder. This would include the various spiritual practices, especially reflection on scripture, and the practical application of such to their own life.

Self-awareness

It would further include an understanding of self-awareness. The elder would need to understand his barriers to spiritual growth and where change is needed, his strengths and weaknesses, and also a sense of humility and vulnerability knowing his dependence on God.

Life Balance

The elder would also need to consider his life balance in terms of his family, work, church involvement, and personal health to be able to maintain a sustained ministry.

Mentoring Others

The elder needs to demonstrate the ability to receive encouragement and rebuke, and that he is willing to be held accountable for his personal walk with Christ. The mentoring in these areas helps the potential elder appreciate what it is he needs to develop in those he is called to oversee and care for.

Further Skills

Further knowledge required or skills that need to be developed would include an overview of the CRCA confessions; basic exegesis and use of the Bible in pastoral care; listening skills, especially reflective listening; mentoring, including one-to-one Bible reading and the use of the G.R.O.W. process; observation skills, including the discernment of a church member's personal issues and theological inclinations; and how to be open about the faith including being able to give their own testimony and share the gospel with others.

Ongoing Accountability

An ongoing accountability and mentoring would be needed for the elders. Even if the elders were trained and involved in the new approach there was the concern that underlying problems of the church members would not be properly discerned by the elder in the small group or, if discerned, not followed up. The minister should be the person to provide the ongoing mentoring of the elders.

Implications for the Ministers

The above has implications for the minister of the local church.

Changed Focus

Ministers need to focus what they do. Pastorally they should not try to provide all the pastoral care in the church. That has become the default position for many ministers. This may be due to elders not doing their role. It is the expectation of the members in many churches that the minister visits all the members regularly. It may be counter-intuitive but more pastoral care would be done if the minister did less of it and focused on the training and mentoring of the elders and the pastoral care workers.

Cautions

Two cautions were noted. The minister could be so tied up with training that he would be exhausted and so he needs to focus eventually on training trainers. The other was that ministers could end up doing no pastoral care. That is not the intent. Ministers would especially be needed for more difficult pastoral concerns. They would also need to continue giving pastoral care to model how it is done with the elders.

Not Competent to Train

There are ministers who did not feel competent to train their elders. In such cases training support from outside the congregation could assist. But it should not be a long-term approach as it is important that the DNA of the church be such that training is naturally part of what it does for its members and leaders.

Changing Session Agendas

Another ramification is that sessions need to seriously reassess what they deal with in their meeting agendas. The focus of the session meetings should be on the spiritual growth of the members such that they are equipped for ministry and the sharing of the gospel in their communities. Non-essential issues should be delegated to others. The elders with their oversight role should determine the overall policy directions and then resource and empower others to take on their tasks. There was a tendency for elders to be involved in committees for finances or the church buildings because it was their natural bent. But elders should not be problem solvers but disciple makers.

Final Remarks

This research has demonstrated that there is a need to rethink how pastoral care is provided by the elders of the CRCA relevant to the circumstances of twenty-first-century Australia. It has also demonstrated a practical method that can empower the local elders to determine what that approach should be in their local setting. This is a very important step in the rejuvenation of the office of elder.

This is a key contribution of this research. It is not being advocated that the approach of pastoral care arrived at in this research is now the only way to go. The broader consultation and critique of the AR makes it clear that there is a great variety of circumstances and approaches in the CRCA. With the rapid changes occurring in our postmodern society any form of pastoral care, including the one devised by the AR, could become ineffective as well.

What is important is that elders and ministers in local churches be given the resources to reflect openly and honestly on their particular circumstances and to use a method like AR to devise what is best practice in their situation. This needs to be encouraged.

There needs to be an understanding of the distinction between form and function. The function of the elder's oversight and pastoral care is well delineated in Scripture. But the form it takes can vary depending on the changed circumstances of such important issues as community, relationships, and how modeling and training is provided.

There is a real need for the church members to be growing in spiritual maturity, that they are using their gifts for ministry in reaching out, such that they develop a passion for the lost. For that to occur it requires a well-functioning eldership as the New Testament envisioned it, not elders who police behavior but who inspire the members by their own example, and who are trained and enthused for their role in the church. We should expect nothing less for those called to be Christ's under-shepherds. It is the prayer and the passion of the researcher that this project will assist in achieving that.

Appendix

Information on the Original Appendices

THE DOCTORAL PROJECT SUBMITTED to the Australian College of Theology contained two very extensive appendices: "Appendix 1 Focus Groups" and "Appendix 2 Action Research." These two appendices had a combined total of over 250,000 words. These appendices provided all the various materials that were designed by the researcher and used in the research as well as the extensive verbatim records and analyses for both the focus groups and the action research that was conducted. The two extensive appendices were included with the thesis so that the reader (especially the doctoral examiners) would be able to "recover" the journey of the research. "Recoverability" is an important aspect of validation in action research. The full details allowed the reader to assess how the researcher functioned in both the focus groups and the action research. It also allowed for independent review of the data to compare that with the analyses and summations made by the researcher.

It was decided, however, for the sake of this publication and its intended readers, that the two appendices in their original state were simply too large to include. Instead a list of all the documents contained in the original appendices is provided so the reader can gain a sense of the extent of the data that was worked with (see below).

For those who wish to review the full set of the original appendices these can be obtained in PDF form by contacting the author at ldouma@crca.org.au or the Administrator, Christian Reformed Churches of Australia at admin@crca.org.au.

List of all Documents Contained in the Original Appendices

FG1 Setting up Focus Groups
- FG1.1 Letter to the Churches
- FG1.2 Church Bulletin Advertisement
- FG1.3 Participant Information
- FG1.4 Consent Forms
- FG1.5 Focus Group Participant's Sheet
- FG1.6 Focus Group Interviewer's Guide
- FG1.7 Acknowledgments

FG2 Verbatim Transcripts of Focus Groups
- FG2.1 Introduction/Acknowledgements
- FG2.2 Summary Data of Participants in Focus Groups
- FG2.3 Verbatim Transcript of Communicant Members Focus Group
- FG2.4 Verbatim Transcript of Elders Focus Group

FG3 Analysis of Focus Groups
- FG3.1 Rationale of Analysis Methodology
- FG3.2 Collation of Responses: Communicant Members Focus Groups
- FG3.3 Collation of Responses: Elder Focus Groups
- FG3.4 Focus Groups Summary Analysis

FG4 International Comparison to Focus Groups
- FG4.1 Notes of Interviews with Christian Reformed Church of North America Ministers

AR1. Action Research Team Meeting 1 (AR1)
- AR1.1 Letter to the Churches
- AR1.2 Consent Forms
- AR1.3 Participant Information
- AR1.4 Details of the AR Elder Participants
- AR1.5 Doctoral Research Proposal
- AR1.6 Research Question

AR1.7 Analysis of the Focus Groups

AR1.8 Summary of the Focus Group Analysis

AR1.9 Statement of Interview of Christian Reformed Church of North America Ministers

AR1.10 Review of the New Testament and Christian Reformed Churches of Australia Confessions re Task of Elders

AR1.11 Methodology Outline of the Action Research Process

AR1.12 How to Keep a Research Diary

AR1.13 Notes of AR1 Meeting August 2, 2009

AR2 Action Research Team Meeting 2 (AR2)

AR2.1 Summary Notes of the AR Team Diaries and Interviews

AR2.2 Elder A Diary Notes

AR2.3 Elder D Diary Notes

AR2.4 Elder F Verbatim Record of Discussion with Researcher

AR2.5 Diary Notes (Researcher)

AR2.6 Notes of Discussion with CRCA Theological Lecturer

AR2.7 Doctoral Paper—"Imaging God—To be Human is to Be in Community"

AR2.8 Doctoral Paper—"Assessing the Model of Discipling by Jesus"

AR2.9 Doctoral paper—"Program for Introducing a Mentoring Component in Your Ministry"

AR2.10 Verbatim Record of AR Team Meeting April 24, 2009

AR3 Action Research Team Meeting 3 (AR3)

AR3.1 Agenda of AR3 Team Meeting

AR3.2 Discussion Point Raised from AR2 Team Meeting

AR3.3 Summary Notes of AR Team Diaries

AR3.4 Elder A Diary Notes

AR3.5 Elder E Diary Notes

AR3.6 Notes/Verbatim Record of AR3 Team Meeting October 12, 2009

AR4 Action Research Team Meeting 4 (AR4)

AR4.1 Agenda of AR4 Team Meeting

AR4.2 Discussion Notes from Elder Diaries

AR4.3 Assignment for the Next Meeting

    AR4.4 Researcher Diary Notes
    AR4.5 Elder A Diary Notes
    AR4.6 Elder B Diary Notes
    AR4.7 Elder E Diary Notes
    AR4.8 Elder F Diary Notes
    AR4.9 Summary of Diaries
    AR4.10 Verbatim Record of AR4 Team Meeting

AR5 Action Research Team Meeting 5 (AR5)
    AR5.1 Paper: Concepts of Spiritual Growth
    AR5.2 Summary of Elders' Diary Notes
    AR5.3 Elder A Diary Notes
    AR5.4 Elder B Diary Notes
    AR5.5 Elder C Diary Notes
    AR5.6 Elder D Diary Notes
    AR5.7 Elder E Diary Notes
    AR5.8 Elder F Diary Notes
    AR5.9 Verbatim Record of AR5 Team Meeting

AR6 Action Research Team Meeting 6 (AR6)
    AR6.1 Agenda of Team Meeting
    AR6.2 Interim Report to Sessions
    AR6.3 Verbatim Record of AR6 Team Meeting

AR7 Action Research Team Meeting 7 (AR7)
    AR7.1 Letter to Ministers/Elders
    AR7.2 Individual Responses/Critique to "Interim Report"
    AR7.3 Verbatim Church A Critique "Interim Report"
    AR7.4 Verbatim Church B Critique "Interim Report"
    AR7.5 Collation of responses/critique to "Interim Report"
    AR7.6 Summary of Responses/Agenda for AR7 Team Meeting
    AR7.7 Verbatim Record of AR7 Team Meeting

Bibliography

Achterstraat, Bert. "She Won't Say Nothing." *Give Yourself to Reading* 8 no. 1 (1966) 9-11.
Adams, Jay E. "Working With the Eldership." *Ordained Servant* 1 no. 2 (1992) 27-29.
Allison, Archibald A. "Visiting the Members." *Ordained Servant* 10 no. 2 (2001) 27-29.
———. "Biblical Qualifications for Elders." *Ordained Servant* 3 no. 2 (1994) 81-96.
Anderson, David F. *The Elder in the Church Today*. Edinburgh: Saint Andrew, 1980.
Askes, Henk. *The Elder in a Troublesome Time for the Church*. Summerville: SC Holy Fire, 2009.
Atkerson, Steve. "The Ministry of Elders." *NTRF Restoring New Testament Practices to Today's Church*. http://www.ntrf.org/articles/article_detail.php?PRKey=2 October 2008.
Barbour, G. F. *The Elder and His Work*. Edinburgh: Saint Andrew, 1980.
Barkley, Alexander. "The Office of Elder." *Give Yourself to Reading* 11 no.3 (1969) 15-21.
Benner, David G. *Care of Souls: Revisioning Christian Nurture and Counsel*. Grand Rapids: Baker, 1998.
Berghoef, Gerard, and Lester DeKoster. *The Elders Handbook: A Practical Guide for Church Leaders*. Grand Rapids: Christian Liberty, 1979.
Bosker, Bill "Training Leaders for the Future." http://www.trowelandsword.org.au/Contents/Back%20Issues/Feature%20Articles/2000s/2009/ArchF200907art1.htm.
Brands, Robert. "The Role of Elders and Deacons in Pastoral Care." *The Standard Bearer* 69 no. 11 (1993) 254-257.
Brown, Juanita, and David Isaacs. *The World Café: Shaping Our Futures Through Conversations that Matter*. San Francisco: Berrett-Koehler, 2005.
Calvin, John. *Institutes of the Christian Religion*. Philadelphia: Westminster, 1973.
Cammenga, Ronald L. "Family Visitation." *The Standard Bearer* 67 no. 4 (1991) 87-88.
———. "Family Visitation (2)." *The Standard Bearer* 67 no. 7 (1991) 151-152.
———. "Warding Off False Doctrines." *The Standard Bearer* 72 no. 6 (1996) 140-141.
———. "Calvin's Struggle for Church Discipline." *The Standard Bearer* 86 no. 3 (2010) 63-65.

Capill, Murray. "Ministry Spot." *RTC Monthly* 19 (2007) 2–3.
———. "Ministry Spot." *RTC Monthly* 20 (2007) 2–3.
———. "Ministry Spot." *RTC Monthly* 21 (2007) 2–3.
———. "Ministry Spot." *RTC Monthly* 22 (2007) 2–3.
———. "Ministry Spot." *RTC Monthly* 23 (2008) 2.
———. "Ministry Spot." *RTC Monthly* 25 (2008) 1–2.
———. "Ministry Spot." *RTC Monthly* 27 (2008) 2.
———. "Ministry Spot." *RTC Monthly* 39 (2010) 2.
Chadwick, Owen. *The Reformation*. Aylesbury: Penguin, 1977.
Champion, Donna, and Frank A. Stowell. "Validating Action Research Field Studies: PEArL." *Systematic Practice and Action Research* 16 no. 1 (2003) 21–36.
Christian Reformed Churches of Australia. *The Provisional Church Order*, Geelong: CRCA Synod, 2000.
Christian Reformed Churches of Australia. *Acts of Synod 2006*. Geelong: CRCA Synod, 2006.
Coghlan, David. "Action Research in the Academy: Why and Whither? Reflections on the Changing Nature of Research." *Irish Journal of Management* 25 no. 2 (2004) 1–10.
Cohen, Louis, and Lawrence Manier. "Action Research." In *Research Methods in Education*, 226–241. London: Routledge, 1994.
Costello, Patrick. *Action Research*. London: Continuum, 2003.
Crane, Phil, and Leanne Richardson. *Reconnect Action Research Kit*. Canberra: Commonwealth Department for Community Services, 2000. http://www.facs.gov.au/sa/housing/pubs/homelessyouth/reconnect-action-research_kit.
Davies, Richard E. *Handbook for Doctor of Ministry Projects: An Approach to Structured Observation of Ministry*. Lanham: University Press of America, 1984.
Dawson, Susan, and Lenore Manderson. *A Manual for the Use of Focus Groups*. Boston: International Nutrition Foundation for Developing Countries, 1993.
Dawson, Susan, et al. *A Manual for the Use of Focus Groups*. Boston: International Nutrition Foundation for Developing Countries, 1992.
De Graaf, Arent I. "What is an Elder, Studies in the Pastoral Letters (1), The Elder's Office." *Give Yourself to Reading* 1 no. 2 (1959) 3–5.
———. "What is an Elder, Studies in the Pastoral Letters (2), The Elder's Background." *Give Yourself to Reading* 1 no. 4 (1959) 8–9.
———. "What is an Elder, Studies in the Pastoral Letters (3), The Elder's Task." *Give Yourself to Reading* 2 no. 1 (1960) 8–10.
———. "What is an Elder, Studies in the Pastoral Letters (4), The Elder's Arsenal." *Give Yourself to Reading* 2 no. 2 (1960) 8–10.
De Jong, Peter Y. *The Church's Witness to the World*. St Catherines: Paideia, 1980.
———. "Taking Heed to the Flock, A Study of the Principles and Practice of Family Visitation Chapter 1: The Name and Nature of Family Visitation." *Ordained Servant* 1 no. 1 (1992) 8–13.
———. "Taking Heed to the Flock, A Study of the Principles and Practice of Family Visitation Chapter 2: The History of Family Visitation." *Ordained Servant* 1 no. 2 (1992) 39–42.
———. "Taking Heed to the Flock, A Study of the Principles and Practice of Family Visitation Chapter 3: The Scriptural Basis of Family Visitation." *Ordained Servant* 1 no. 3 (1992) 56–62.

———. "Taking Heed to the Flock, A Study of the Principles and Practice of Family Visitation Chapter 4: The Spiritual Purpose of Family Visitation." *Ordained Servant* 2 no. 1 (1993) 19–22.

———. "Taking Heed to the Flock, A Study of the Principles and Practice of Family Visitation Chapter 5: The Necessity of Family Visitation." *Ordained Servant* 2 no. 2 (1993) 38–41.

———. "Taking Heed to the Flock, A Study of the Principles and Practice of Family Visitation Chapter 6: The Requisites for Family Visitation." *Ordained Servant* 2 no. 3 (1993) 65–69.

———. "Taking Heed to the Flock, A Study of the Principles and Practice of Family Visitation Chapter 7: Objections to Family Visitation." *Ordained Servant* 2 no. 4 (1993) 86–90.

———. "Taking Heed to the Flock, A Study of the Principles and Practice of Family Visitation Chapter 8: The Value of Family Visitation." *Ordained Servant* 3 no. 1 (1994) 18–22.

———. "Taking Heed to the Flock, A Study of the Principles and Practice of Family Visitation Chapter 9: The Proper Practice of Family Visitation." *Ordained Servant* 3 no. 2 (1994) 35–41.

———. "Taking Heed to the Flock, A Study of the Principles and Practice of Family Visitation. Chapter 10: The Supreme Ideal of Family Visitation." *Ordained Servant* 3 no. 3 (1994) 51–52.

———. "The Elders Rule." *Give Yourself to Reading* 12 no. 3 (1970) 22–25.

De Koning, Neil. "Christian Maturity & the Call of the Elder." http://network.crcna.org/content/elders/christian-maturity-call-elder.

———."Do I Have What It Takes?" http://network.crcna.org/content/elders/do-i-have-what-it-takes.

———. "Elder Visitation Record." http://network.crcna.org/content/elders/elder-visitation-recorddoc.

———. "Elders and Spiritual Formation." http://network.crcna.org/content/elders/elders-and-spiritual-formation.

———. "Getting Started as a First-Time Elder." http://network.crcna.org/content/elders/egetting-started-first-time-elder.

———. *Guiding the Faith Journey: A Map for Spiritual Leaders*. Grand Rapids: CRC, 1996.

———. "Home Visit." http://network.crcna.org/forums/elders/elders-general-discussion/home-visit.

———. "Just-in-Time Learning." http://network.crcna.org/content/elders/just-time-learning.

———. "Member Involvement Letter." http://network.crcna.org/content/elders/member-invovlement-letterdoc.

———. "The Various Roles of an Elder" http://network.crcna.org/content/elders/elder-various-roles-elder.

De Moor, Henry. "Job Sharing Among Elders." http://network.crcna.org/content/elders/job-sharing-among-elders.

De Ridder, Richard R. *In His Service: Family Visitation*. Grand Rapids: CRC, 1987.

———. *In His Service: The Special Offices of the Church*. Grand Rapids: CRC, 1987.

De Ruiter, Gerrit. "The Elder and His Work." *Give Yourself to Reading* 6 no. 1 (1964) 8–11.

———. "The Precious Art of Listening." *Give Yourself to Reading* 6 no. 2 (1964) 7–10.

———. "The Elder and Young Folk." *Give Yourself to Reading* 6 no. 4 (1964) 13–15.

———. "Mr Elder in Conference with Himself." *Give Yourself to Reading* 8 no. 1 (1966) 15–18.

Decker, Robert D. "The Elders and Family Visitation." *The Standard Bearer* 75 no. 5 (1999) 105–106.

Dekker, James C. "Hints for Visiting." http://network.crcna.org/content/pastors/hints-visiting.

Dever, Mark. *A Display of God's Glory, Basics of Church Structure. Deacons, Elders, Congregationalism and Membership*. Washington: 9Marks Ministries, 2001.

———, and Alexander, Paul. *The Deliberate Church: Building Your Ministry on the Gospel*. Wheaton: Crossway, 2005.

Dick, Bob. "Action Learning and Action Research." http://www.scu.edu.au/schools/gcm/ar/arp/actlearn.html.

———. "Action Research: Action and Research." http://www.scu.edu.au/schools/gcm/or/arp/aandr.html.

———. "Questions for Critical Reflection." http://www.scu.edu.au./schools/gcm/ar/arp/reflques.html.

———. "Structured Focus Groups." http://www.scu.edu.au/schools/gcm/ar/arp/focus.html.

Douma, Leo. "The Challenge of New Leadership and Governance Theories on Reformed Church Governance." Doctor of Ministry paper, Australian College of Theology, 2005.

———. "Imaging God: To be Human is to be in Community." Doctor of Ministry paper, Australian College of Theology, 2006.

———. "Assessing the Model of Discipling by Jesus." Doctor of Ministry paper, Australian College of Theology, 2007.

———. "Program for Introducing a Mentoring Component in your Ministry." Doctor of Ministry paper, Australian College of Theology, 2007.

Driscoll, Mark. *On Church Leadership*. Wheaton: Crossway, 2008.

Eagan, Toby M., and Cynthia M. Lancaster, "Comparing Appreciative Inquiry to Action Research: OD Practitioner Perspectives." *Organization Development Journal* 23 no. 2 (Summer 2005) 29–49.

Elliot, John. *Action Research for Educational Change*. Buckingham: Open University Press, 1998.

Esselbrugge, Albert. "From the Manse." *Church Letter of the Reformed Church of Box Hill*, Box Hill: Box Hill Reformed Church, September 9 2007.

Evans, Dirk. "Correcting a Structural Heresy." *The Banner* (2006). www.thebanner.org/magazine/article.cfm?article_id=653.

Eyres, Lawrence R. *The Elders of the Church*. Phillipsburg: New Jersey Presbyterian and Reformed, 1975.

Fennema, C. Eric. "On Doing Home Visitation." *Ordained Servant* 7 no. 2 (1998) 32–34.

Firet, Jacob. *Dynamics in Pastoring*. Grand Rapids: Eerdmans, 1986.

Foster, Michael. "An Introduction to the Theory and Practice of Action Research in Work Organizations." *Human Relations* 25 no. 6 (1972) 529–56.

Getz, Gene A. *Sharpening the Focus of the Church*. Illinois: Victor, 1984.

Goodliff, Paul. *Care in a Confused Climate: Pastoral Care and Postmodern Culture*. Grand Rapids: Darton, Longman & Todd, 1998.

Greenwood, Davydd, J., and Morten Levin. *Introduction to Action Research* (2nd ed.) Thousand Oaks: SAGE, 2007.
Gritters, Barry. "Elders Who Know Their Sheep." *The Standard Bearer* 76 no. 13 (2000) 300–302.
Groenenboom, David. "Growing Real Leaders." http://wwwtrowelandsword.org.au/rsclead200008art1.htm.
———. "Thinking About Leadership." http://wwwtrowelandsword.org.au/rsclead200202art1.htm.
———. "Pastoral Care in the Community." http://wwwtrowelandsword.org.au/contents/back%20issues/feature%20issues%20articles.
Hammond, Sue A. *The Thin Book of Appreciative Inquiry*. Plano: Thin Book, 1998.
Hanko, Herman. *Notes on the Church Order*. Grand Rapids: Theological School of the Protestant Reformed Churches, 1973.
———. "The Calling of Elders." *The Standard Bearer* 61 no. 13 (1985) 295–300.
Hawkins, Greg L., and Cathy Parkinson. *Reveal: Where Are You?* Barrington: Willow Creek, 2007.
———. *Reveal: A Spiritual Growth Conversation, Follow Me, What's Next for You?* Barrington: Willow Creek, 2008.
Herr, Katherine, and Gary Anderson. *The Action Research Dissertation: A Guide for Students and Faculty*. London: SAGE, 2005.
Hilbelink, John R. "A Training Course for Elders and Deacons, In Two Sections." *Ordained Servant* 2 no. 1 (1993) 3–15.
———. "A Training Course for Elders and Deacons, In Two Sections." *Ordained Servant* 2 no. 2 (1993) 27–37.
Hoeksema, Herman. "Family Visitation." *Protestant Reformed Theological Journal* 6 no. 1. (1972) 25–55.
Holian, Rosalie. "Doing Research in My Own Organisation: Ethical Dilemmas, Hopes and Triumphs." http://www.scu.edu.au/schools/gcm/ar/ari/p-rholian99.html.
Hoving, Harry.L. "The Elder as Pastor. Home Visits." *Elders and Deacons at Work, Guidelines for Office Bearers in the Reformed Churches*. Geelong: Reformed Churches, 1982.
Hughes, Irfon. "In the Church-Visit and Prosper." http://www.byfaithonline.com/CC/CDA/Content_Blocks/CC_Printer_Friendly-Version.
Hyde, Daniel R. "The Duties of Elders." *Ordained Servant* 13 no. 1 (2004) 4–7.
Keeley, Robert J., ed. *Shaped by God, Twelve Essentials for Nurturing Faith in Children, Youth and Adults*. Grand Rapids: Faith Alive Christian Resources, 2010.
Kemmis, Stephen, and Robin McTaggart. *The Action Research Planner*. Geelong, Deakin University Press, 1988.
Kleinjan, M. "Talks from an Elder to Elders: The Elder and His Duty." *Give Yourself to Reading* 6 no. 4 (1964) 19–21.
Knox OPC. "Knox Voters' Guide, Knox Orthodox Presbyterian Church, Silver Spring, Maryland 1991." *Ordained Servant* 1 no. 3 (1992) 51–58.
Kok, James R. *90% of Helping is Just Showing Up*. Grand Rapids: CRC, 1996.
Kortering, Jason L. "Family Worship: A Reformed Heritage." *The Standard Bearer* 55 no. 2 (1979). 41–43.
Koshy, Valsa. *Action Research for Improving Practice: A Practical Guide*. London: Paul Chapman, 2005.

Krueger, Richard A. *Analysing and Reporting Focus Group Results*. Thousand Oaks: SAGE, 1998.

Kuiper, Douglas. "Called to Serve: Essays for Elders and Deacons." http://standardbearer.rfpa.org/articles/called-serve-essays-elders-and-deacons.

Langerak, William. "Called to Serve: Essays for Elders and Deacons." *The Standard Bearer* 86 no. 1 (1997) 21–22.

Larson, Mark. "A Reformed Perspective of Home Visitation." *Ordained Servant* 4 no. 2 (1995) 38–40.

Leech, Kenneth. *Spirituality and Pastoral Care*. London: Sheldon, 1987.

Lund, Torbjorn. *Understanding the Role of the Action Researcher in Dialogue Conferences*. Oslo: Tromso University, 2005. http://www.ped.gu.se/kollegier/aktionsforskning/TorbjornLundspaper.pdf.

MacDonald, William C. *The Elder: His Character and Duties*. Edinburgh: St Andrews, 1958.

Maguire, Patricia. "Challenges, Contradictions and Celebrations: Attempting Participatory Research as a Doctoral Student." In *Voices of Change: Participatory Research in the United States and Canada*, 157–76. Toronto: OISE, 1993.

Mason, John. *Researching Your Own Practice: The Discipline of Noticing*. London: Routledge, 2002.

McKee, Elsie A. "The Offices of Elders and Deacons in the Classical Reformed Tradition." In *Major Themes in the Reformed Tradition*, 344–353. Grand Rapids: Eerdmans, 1992.

McNamara, Carter. "Basics of Conducting Focus Groups." http://managementhelp.org/evaluatn/focusgrp/htm.

McNeill, John T. *The History and Character of Calvinism*. New York: Oxford University Press, 1973.

McNiff, Jean. *Action Research in Organizations*. London: Routledge, 2000.

———. *Action Research, Principles and Practice*. New York: RoutledgeFalmer, 2002.

———. and Jack Whitehead. *Action Research: Principles and Practice*. Abingdon: RoutledgeFalmer, 2007.

Meehan, Charlie and Coghlan, David. "Developing Managers as Healing Agents in Organizations: A Co-operative Inquiry Approach." *Systematic Practice and Action Research* 17 no. 5 (2004). 407–408.

Meyer, Charlie. "Eldership in the Balance." *Ordained Servant* 10 no. 2 (2001) 312–34.

Ministry Tools Resource Centre. "Shepherding Ministry Venue: Elders." http://mintools.com/elders.htm.

Morgan, David L. *Focus Groups as Qualitative Research*. Newbury Park: SAGE, 1988.

Myers, William R. *Research in Ministry: A Primer for the Doctor of Ministry Program*. Chicago: Exploration, 2002.

Australian Government. *National Statement on Ethical Conduct in Research Involving Humans*. Canberra: Commonwealth of Australia, 2005.

O'Brien, Rory. "An Overview of the Methodological Approach of Action Research." http:/www.web-nwt/~robrien/papers/arfinal.html.

Oak, John H. *Healthy Christians Make a Healthy Church*. Fearn: Christian Focus, 2003.

Osborne, Larry. *The Sticky Church*. Grand Rapids: Zondervan, 2008.

Osterhaven, M. Eugene. *Our Confession of Faith: A Study Manual on the Belgic Confession*. Grand Rapids: Baker Book House, 1967.

Piper, John. "Biblical Eldership, Part 1a." http://www.desiringgod.org/messages/biblical-eldership-part-1a.

———. "Christian Elders in the New Testament." http://www.desiringgod.org/articles/christian-elders-in-the-new-testament.

Pope, Randy. *The Intentional Church: Moving from Church Success to Community Transformation*. Chicago: Moody, 2006.

Pugh, Jeff. *Action Research Method Notes*. Unpublished work. Lilydale: Bible College of Victoria, 2008.

———. *Appreciative Inquiry Notes*. Unpublished work. Lilydale: Bible College of Victoria, 2008.

Reformed Churches of Australia. *Book of Forms*. Geelong: Reformed Churches, 1991.

Relationships Forum. *An Unexpected Tragedy: Evidence for the Connection between Working Patterns and Family Breakdown in Australia*. www.relationshipsforum.org.au.

Reynolds, Greg, and William Shishko. "A Training Program for Elders." *Ordained Servant* 10 no. 3 (2001) 55–58.

Sankaran, Shankar. "Action Research Bibliography." http://www.scu.edu.au/schools/gcm/ar/arp/al-biblio.

Sarantakos, Sotirios. *Social Research*. South Yarra: MacMillan, 1998.

Scazzero, Peter. *The Emotionally Healthy Church: A Strategy for Discipleship that Actually Changes Lives*. Grand Rapids: Zondervan, 2003.

Schaver, John Louis L. *The Polity of the Churches V2*. Grand Rapids: International, 1961.

Schep, J. A. "The Biblical Requirements for Office Bearers." *Give Yourself to Reading* 9 no. 4 (1967) 10–11.

———."The Biblical Requirements for Office Bearers II." *Give Yourself to Reading* 10 no. 1 (1968) 11–13.

———. "The Biblical Requirements for Office Bearers III." *Give Yourself to Reading* 10 no. 2 (1968) 16–18.

———. "The Biblical Requirements for Office Bearers IV." *Give Yourself to Reading* 10 no. 3 (1968) 7–9.

———. "The Biblical Requirements for Office Bearers V." *Give Yourself to Reading* 10 no. 4 (1968) 7–9.

———. "The Biblical Requirements for Office Bearers VI." *Give Yourself to Reading* 11 no. 1 (1969) 4–7.

Scipione, George C. *Timothy, Titus and You. A Workbook for Church Leaders*. Chattanooga: Pilgrim, 1975.

Seidman, Irving. *Interviewing as Qualitative Research: A Guide for Researchers in Education and the Social Sciences*. New York: Teachers College, 1998.

Senneker, J. "Talks from an Elder to Elders." *Give Yourself to Reading* 5 no. 1 (1963) 19–20.

Shannon, Sharkur. *Effective Change Management Using Action Learning and Action Research: Concepts, Frameworks, Process Applications*. Lismore: Southern Cross University Press, 2001.

Sietsma, K. *The Idea of Office*. Jordan Station, Ontario: Paideia, 1985.

Sittema, John R. "Specific Help for Elder Visiting." *Ordained Servant* 5 no. 2 (1996) 28–30.

———. "Some Thoughts on Term Eldership." *Ordained Servant* 10 no. 2 (2001) 35–37.

Sittema, John R. *With a Shepherd's Heart: Reclaiming the Pastoral Office of Elder.* Grandville: Reformed Fellowship, 1996.

Sittema, John. "Pastoring With a Purpose." *The Outlook* 52 no. 5 (2002) 14–16.

Stairs, Jean. *Listening for the Soul: Pastoral Care and Spiritual Direction.* Minneapolis: Augsburg Fortress, 2000.

Steere, David A., ed. *The Supervision of Pastoral Care.* Louisville: Westminster/John Knox, 1989.

Stewart, David W., and Prem N. Shamdasani, *Focus Group: Theory and Practice.* Newbury Park: SAGE, 1990.

———, and Dennis, W. Rook. *Focus Group: Theory and Practice*, Second Edition. Thousand Oaks: SAGE, 2007.

Strauch, Alexander. *Biblical Eldership: An Urgent Call to Restore Biblical Leadership.* Littleton: Lewis and Roth, 1995.

———. *Biblical Eldership: Restoring the Eldership to its Rightful Place in the Church.* Littleton: Lewis and Roth, 1997.

———. *The Mentor's Guide to Biblical Eldership: Twelve Lessons for Mentoring Men for Eldership.* Littleton: Lewis and Roth, 1996.

Strauss, Anselm L. *Qualitative Analysis for Social Scientists.* Cambridge: Cambridge University Press, 2003.

Swart, Martin. "The Proper Manner of Conducting Family Visitation." *The Standard Bearer* 73 no. 7 (1997) 164–167.

Tamminga, Louis M. *A Handbook for Elders: Guiding God's People in a Changing World.* Grand Rapids: CRC, 1998.

———. *The Elder's Handbook.* Grand Rapids: Faith Alive Christian Resources, 2009.

Tanner, Ian B. *A Handbook for Elders Within the Uniting Church in Australia.* Melbourne: Uniting Church of Australia, 1984.

Taylor, Allison. "Theological Leadership in Pastoral Care." In *Making Connections: Theological Leadership and the Australian Church.* Sydney: Anglican General Synod, 2001. www.anglican.org.au/docs/MakingConnections.

Ten Clay, Tim. "Comments on: Elders and Huis Bezoek." http://tenclay.org/blog/2006/01/19/elders-huis-bezoek/feed/.

Thompson, Frank, and Chad Perry. "Generalising Results of an Action Research Project in One Work Place to Other Situations." *European Journal of Marketing* 38 no. 3/4 (2004) 401–417.

Torrance, T. F. *The Eldership in the Reformed Church.* Edinburgh: Handsel, 1984.

Trice, T. N. "The Ingredients of a Successful Oversight Program." *Ordained Servant* 10 no. 3 (2001) 46–50.

Unknown. "Eighteen Reasons for Elders to do Home Visitation." *Ordained Servant* 13 no. 4 (2004) 92.

———. "Pointers for Elders and Deacons: Part 1 of an Article from the DIAKONIA, Translated from the Dutch Language" *Ordained Servant* 2 no. 3 (1993) 59–64.

———. "Pointers for Elders and Deacons: Part 2 of an Article from the DIAKONIA, Translated from the Dutch Language" *Ordained Servant* 2 no. 4 (1993) 79–85.

———. "Pointers for Elders and Deacons: Part 3 of an Article from the DIAKONIA, Translated from the Dutch Language" *Ordained Servant* 3 no. 1 (1994) 3–9.

Van Brussel, Willem F. "Are you Really Aware that You Are an Office Bearer." *Give Yourself to Reading* 2 no. 4 (1960) 10–12.

———. "Questions of Our Elders." *Give Yourself to Reading* 3 no. 4 (1961) 14–15.

———. "Our Reaction." *Give Yourself to Reading* 7 no. 3 (1965) 5–10.
———. "Pastoral Care by Elders." *Give Yourself to Reading* 11 no. 3 (1969) 22–25.
———. "Pastoral Care by Elders: Authority in Their Calls." *Give Yourself to Reading* 11 no. 4 (1969) 3–7.
———. "Pastoral Care by Elders." *Give Yourself to Reading* 12 no. 1 (1970) 17–20.
———. "Home Visitation: How Should We Do It?" *Give Yourself to Reading* 12 no. 2 (1969) 3–8.
———. "Pastoral Care." *Give Yourself to Reading* 12 no. 3 (1970) 3–9.
———. "Elders' Conference in Victoria." *Give Yourself to Reading* 13 no. 2 (1971) 4–12.
———. "The Elder's Office in Scripture and History." In *Elders and Deacons at Work, Guidelines for Office Bearers in the Reformed Churches*, 7–21. Geelong: Reformed Churches Publishing House, 1982.
Van Dam, Cornelis. *The Elder: Today's Ministry Rooted in All of Scripture*. Phillipsburg, New Jersey: P&R, 2009.
Van Dellen, Idzerd, and Martin Monsma. *The Church Order Commentary: Being a Brief Explanation of the Church Order of the Christian Reformed Church*. Grand Rapids: Zondervan, 1941.
Van Rougen, G. *Decently and in Order: The Church Order of Dortrecht as Raised by the Synod of Kelmscott 1983 of the Free Reformed Churches of Australia*. Kelmscott: Pro Ecclesia, 1986.
Vander Bom, John. "Are Elders to be Examined?" *Give Yourself to Reading* 2 no. 4 (1960) 3–6.
———. "The Man of God." *Give Yourself to Reading* 3 no. 2 (1961) 3–5.
Vander Pyl, Dick G. "Talks from and Elder to Elders: The Elder Through Many Eyes." *Give Yourself to Reading* 5 no. 4 (1963) 14–17.
———. *Church Order Commentary of the Reformed Churches of New Zealand*. Hamilton, New Zealand: National Publishing Committee of the Reformed Churches of New Zealand, 1992.
———. *Office Bearers' Handbook: Containing Decisions of the Reformed Churches of New Zealand through 1992*. Upper Hutt, New Zealand: National Publishing Committee of the Reformed Churches of New Zealand, 1992.
———. "Elder to Elder: How Important is Faithful Family Visitation?" *Ordained Servant* 8 no. 2 (1999) 32–35.
Vander Staal, John. "Joy in Office." *Give Yourself to Reading* 5 no. 1 (1963) 10–13.
Vanderwell, Howard, D. *Now That You are an Elder*. Fullerton: R. C. Law, 1990.
Wadsworth, Yoland. "What is Participatory Action Research?" *Action Research International*. http://www.scu.edu/schools/gcm/ari/p-ywadsorth98.html.
Walker, Williston. *A History of the Christian Church*. Edinburgh: T&T Clark, 1970.
Warren, Rick. *The Purpose Driven Church: Growth Without Compromising Your Message and Mission*. Grand Rapids: Zondervan, 1995.
Webb, Andrew. "On Pastoral Visitation." http://biblebased.wordpress.com/2007/10/04/on-pastoral-visitation/.
Wesseling, Jay. "What is an Elder to do?" *Give Yourself to Reading* 11 no. 1 (1969) 17–20.
———. "What is an Elder to do? II." *Give Yourself to Reading* 11 no. 2 (1969) 22–24.
Whitney, Diana, and Amanda Trolste-Bloom. *The Power of Appreciative Inquiry: A Practical Guide to Positive Change*. San Francisco: Berret-Koehler, 2003.
Wilkinson, Mervyn. *Action Research for People and Organizational Change*. Brisbane: Queensland University of Technology, 1996.

Williamson, G. I. "A Look at the Biblical Offices." *Ordained Servant* 1 no. 2 (1992) 30–38.

———. "The Importance of Home Visitation." *Ordained Servant* 18 (2009) 31–33.

———. "How to Get Started." *Ordained Servant* 1 no. 1 (1992) 5–7.

Wilson, Larry. "Indians, Farmers and Church Officers." *Ordained Servant* 5 no. 4 (1996) 79–80.

Winslow, David. "Elder to Elder: Start Those Home Visits Now!" *Ordained Servant* 7 no. 1 (1998) 20–21.

———. "A Sample Sessional Calling Card." *Ordained Servant* 7 no. 2 (1998) 29–31.

———. "Elder to Elder: Home Visitation and Family Devotions." *Ordained Servant* 8 no. 1 (1999) 19–20.

Worrel, Tim. "Elders in Pastoral Visitation." *Ordained Servant* 6 no. 3 (1997) 71.

Zwaan, L. "Home Visitation." *Give Yourself to Reading* 8 no. 4 (1966) 12–15.

www.ingramcontent.com/pod-product-compliance
Lightning Source LLC
Chambersburg PA
CBHW050836160426
43192CB00010B/2047